Private Pain in Public Pews

Dr. Elaine A. Bour Spencer

NOV 2010.

Private Pain in Public Pews

Uncovering the Hidden Secrets of Life in the Pews

Dr. Elaine A. Brown Spencer

WestBow
PRESS
A DIVISION OF THOMAS NELSON

WestBow Press books may be ordered through booksellers or by contacting:

WestBow Press
A Division of Thomas Nelson
1663 Liberty Drive
Bloomington, IN 47403
www.westbowpress.com
1-(866) 928-1240

Because of the dynamic nature of the Internet, any Web addresses or links contained in this book may have changed since publication and may no longer be valid. The views expressed in this work are solely those of the author and do not necessarily reflect the views of the publisher, and the publisher hereby disclaims any responsibility for them.

Any people depicted in stock imagery provided by Thinkstock are models, and such images are being used for illustrative purposes only.

Certain stock imagery © Thinkstock.

ISBN: 978-1-4497-0616-6 (sc)
ISBN: 978-1-4497-0617-3 (dj)
ISBN: 978-1-4497-0615-9 (e)

Library of Congress Control Number: 2010938166

Scripture quotations marked (NLT) are taken from the Holy Bible, New Living Translation, copyright © 1996, 2004, 2007. Used by permission of Tyndale House Publishers, Inc., Carol Stream, Illinois 60188. All rights reserved.

The King James Bible. (1988). Nashville: Thomas Nelson Publishers.

Printed in the United States of America

WestBow Press rev. date: 10/12/2010

This book is dedicated to my husband, Floid N. Spencer and my three children, Camille, Andrae & Chrystal for their unconditional support, patience and love.

To every person that helped to inspire this book - thank you.

May the peace of God be with you forever.

Contents

Prologue

In April 2010, I received a dictation from the Lord. It came following an intervention with one of God's children who had been battling past trauma in secret. As I and another minister of the Lord spoke to this person and helped to facilitate healing from the Lord, I left the scene and was unable to sleep for the entire night.

The next morning, I relived the events of the previous evening and on a bus, the Lord began to speak to me. I was told to put pen to paper and write specific things that would help the individual to connect the dots of their life. The words that came from the Lord were words of knowledge that brought clarity to help this person through their deliverance. As the Lord instructed me to write, I literally could not stop. The words He spoke in my spirit that day cascaded out of me like a waterfall.

Chapter 1 is a letter to Rahab as dictated through the Holy Spirit. The story of Rahab can be found in Joshua, chapter 2. This woman, a known prostitute, had provided safe haven for the men sent by Joshua to spy on the land. In her kind deed to help these men she asked them in verse 12:

> Now therefore I pray you, swear unto me by the Lord, since
> I have shewed you kindness, that ye will also shew kindness
> unto my father's house and give me a true token.

These words that Rahab spoke were a prophetic utterance that erased her state of prostitution. Her bloodline could be traced to Jesus, which tells us that regardless of our situation or condition, we can have a future that is bright.

Rahab represents many individuals in the church today, individuals in our church pews who have suffered from childhood abuse, parental abandonment, mental illness, sexual sins and family breakdown. Pain that is experienced in the pew is screaming for attention. Through the intervention for this one life, the Holy Spirit has allowed me to hear the screams of many. These screams have been silent for too long. It is time we not only hear these screams but apply a remedy. Jesus Christ is our only hope. *Private Pain in Public Pews* is removing the mask from the pews. It is important that you understand that no matter what you have been through or whatever you have done, God can heal your pain.

What follows in this chapter was written through the inspiration of the Lord. What I thought was a one-to-one intervention for one of God's precious children has become an intervention for the masses. So be it, Lord.

By faith the harlot Rahab perished not with them that believed not, when she had received the spies with peace.
Hebrews 11:31

Chapter 1

A Letter to Rahab

The Lord has found you in your state. It is you. I speak to you to speak through others. I connect you with those where my healing power can be reciprocated. It is you I want to reaffirm who you are by doing so you affirm others. The word that came through my servant was that it can be reciprocated unto you. The scarlet thread is being applied. Be made whole. Apply it in your womb and tell your womb it shall bring forth. Reverse every word you spoke against your womb and speak life. Be Made Whole.

All the abuse of your past is revealed for you to be free of it. No more shame, no more silence. No more. Speak it, expose it, vomit it out. Tell them no more am I hostage of the affliction, distance memories, childhood traumas, parental disconnects, bloodlines sin, no more. I speak it, I acknowledge it, and I am no more a part of it.

You are not who they say you are. You mean well for others. The stigma of your family, your mistakes of the past has been a buffet. Let them go. Check your bloodline again, Rahab. You have connected with your biological bloodline and fulfilled their negative transferences. You are not of that bloodline. Rahab the harlot has been stigmatized. She gave her body away but she was chosen to carry the promised seed the Messiah! Her name is written in the archives of faith, printed in the pages of the heavenly book for all to know despite her earthly identification and what others thought of her – God used her mightily as he will do for you.

The person you went after, the person you gave your body to. The individual who still is lodged in the channels of your mind and emotions, Let them Go. You have repented but you have not forgiven you. Beneath the Outward dressing of clothing, you are not clothed because your shame, low self-worth, lack of desire for life has held you hostage. Cut the negativities out of you – bring understanding to this situation.

Unlock it, speak it renounce it.

The three words you wanted to hear "I am sorry." Everyone that has done you wrong, everyone that left you to bleed and die hear these words "I Am Sorry." God has forgiven you, He has pulled you out. You will not be exposed. If it is exposed, it will not be you but through an unrepented vessel that refuses to change.

Love yourself because you are beautiful. You have not had your best meal yet. Start eating – order dessert? Practise your smile. Scrape money together and go on vacation. Enjoy life. Ask God what you want. Let your requests be made known unto God. Your appetite for earthly food and heavenly food has returned. Buy books and study the word of God. You will Minister to people you never dreamed of. Sound the alarm. Where you physically cannot go your words and deliverance in life will reach the masses.

He has given you beauty for ashes. Go! Go! Go! You are not silent anymore. You can talk about your experiences with no regret, with no pain, with no bondage. Be Free, Be made Whole, Loose people near and far.

You have found my precious servants, Rahab. Who had similar yet distinct pain. The spiritual authorization has come through you. Mighty (Wo)Man of Valour! Once you are fully made whole you will go distances in God.

You will be exposed to faces you have never known. With boldness will you intercede for others. Your voice will be imprinted in the minds of people. Be Careful! Be Diligent! Be Consecrated! Be Courageous in speaking things and going into the areas where there is silent pain that has never been revealed. Spread the word! Speak into the lives and souls of people. All souls are mine, says the Lord.

Psalms 35:1 "Plead my cause oh Lord with them that strive with me: fight against them that fight against me. Take hold of shield and buckler, and stand up for mine help". Learn this passage. You will stand your ground when others speak against you. The spirit has revealed that there were people in your life that used information in manipulative ways. They cannot help you. I will help them. I will admonish them. I will teach them. I will heal them. That knife that was put in your back – take the shield of faith. Cover yourself with the armour of God. Wounds are markers for experience and your character to be built. I know you love them and respect them but leave them to my will. They speak to me and they know their flaws. Everyone is learning. Everyone is building. The right individuals are placed nearby to witness the blossoming of your future.

Those individuals of your past that is difficult to let go. What did they really mean to you? Speak to why you can't sever that relationship. This seems to be a tender area. Why? I know, but do you know? You are higher than the men you've known. Pull away, delete numbers, and block numbers as you have been instructed to do.

Read my word in Zechariah 3:1-10: "Take away the filthy garments. He has caused thine iniquity to pass from thee and I will cloth you with a change of raiment." Where do you really see yourself professionally? Think this through. Activate both your spiritual and physical ambitions. You must always work with people. Your imprint is long lasting. That is why everyone always wants to be a part of your world. Everyone wants to know what you will say and do.

Work on your critical mind. Use the way you think to be critical of Spirits not People. Because your mind is impressionable due to your gifting it also can be an avenue to re-hash thoughts and feelings that the enemy can use to conjure negativity.

Let those you have associated with repent on their own. I see all, I know all. Esau sought repentance with tears but it was not found. It is a heart condition, a contrition, a roundabout turn. I will know.

The servant who has come to you has been enrolled in my university – my spiritual university. It is a quick work. I have endowed Divine Intelligence. Spirit of Wisdom and Understanding, Spirit of Counsel and Might, Spirit of Knowledge and the Fear of the Lord. I have taught her to wait upon me for instruction. She has asked me what her role is for your life. She seeks for the purity of this spiritual intervention. I ask her to write and echo the words of the servant who delivered this word unto you – not just for you – but for other people. You have never spoken before – there were no safe places to do it. When you went through the hurt and pain of a severed relationship it was part of me schooling you how to be authentic, honest and pruned to do the will of God. The writer had to get her integrity restored, to know how to minister and keep information of people that is private. She will not use information for self-aggrandizement but to be my inspired writer, to put pen on pages to document what life experiences look like and how one can overcome.

She asked me in the heat of a severed relationship to go to those who hurt her, but I restrained her in one instance. She obeyed, prayed through it until I knew she was ready to be healed. If she had gone to them when she wanted to go, this divine appointment could not have taken shape. She has been entrusted with the "skill of understanding." Gabriel gave this to Daniel, she needs this to write the vision and make it plain. She writes to show you my intents. It is safe to speak. She is a caretaker because your life, Rahab, has been chosen for her to bridge gaps, hurts, successes in God. To write books, speak in conferences and affect the masses. How similar you are. Cherish what is divine and don't corrupt the spiritual with the natural. Pray that she will be continuously inspired to broach areas few have been able to do. Speak as the Lord lead you.

From,

The Inspiration of the Holy Ghost

*He that hath an ear, let him hear what the Spirit
saith unto the churches.
(Revelations 2:11, KJV)*

Chapter 2

Real Talk

The challenges we face in life seem at times to be more than we can bear. Unfortunately, the one place where we ought to find solace, peace and healing has too often become little more than a Sunday morning soap opera. We in the church present an image that everything is okay, but if we "lift up the carpet", we see "a whole heap of mess underneath". People in the church are struggling to keep it together. Church folk have masterfully taken on false identities that feed the religious community's expectations of the church, while draining them of who they really are. This creates the ingredients for a downward spiral, where people try to amputate their pain from their reality. In this chapter I will engage in "real talk," which is a no-nonsense conversation about what we know but don't want to talk about. "Real talk" is the story that has not been told. This is not an attempt to air our dirty laundry, so to speak, but to *wash it clean* by acknowledging that there is a problem.

The testimony service that was once tantamount to a public victory proclamation is becoming an endangered species within modern churches. Sadly, it has been replaced by hidden testimonies, not of victories, but of failures experienced behind church walls. These hidden testimonies are not heard in a church service accompanied by songs of praise; they are heard in private discussions and whispers about the lives of saints who have allegedly fallen. Those real testimonies have been archived in the silent screams of church members. The problem is that, because we prefer our own versions of the story, we are not tuning in to the real talk that exists behind the screams. As a result, many of the public displays of infidelity, embezzlement and scandal are never understood in context. Secret acts of indiscretion that have not gone public have stories behind them too—stories that we've never heard.

Too often, church folk are like fish in a bowl who have become so accustomed to their environment that they don't notice which of them are being fed or underfed. One day, all they see is one of their fellows floating at the top of the tank, no longer able to live in its environment. Many church folk today have not been properly fed and so have ceased to thrive in their habitat. Too often, they manage to go unnoticed—until they are belly-up on the surface.

What if we were to pause to learn the story that is never told? Could we retrain ourselves to *think* before jumping to conclusions about those caught up in sin, scandal or an unexplained event? In the next few pages, I will introduce some folks who may remind us of real-life members in our churches—members we all may have heard about. A deeper look into the lives of these fictitious characters can help us to connect some dots as to what is going on all around us. But, before we hear the characters' real talk, let's listen in on some whispers and testimonies about them.

> "Did you hear what happened to Minister Terry? The word on the street is, they saw him uptown in a hotel with Deacon Gregory's twenty-two-year-old daughter. You'd never believe how the word got out. My cousin's mother-in-law—she came to Easter service last year—well, she works in the hospitality department at that uptown hotel. She recognized Minister Terry because he shook her hand when she came to church and welcomed her as a first-time visitor. She especially remembered him because the church made him stand up in the congregation to wish him and his wife happy anniversary. Anyway, she was working at the hotel and when she went to change the towels in the room, who did she see coming out the room with Minister Terry but Deacon Gregory's daughter! He didn't even recognize my cousin's mother-in-law, but, oh, she recognized him! By the way, Minister Terry preached an awesome sermon last Sunday."

"Now, don't tell anybody, but I heard that Samantha and her Sunday school teacher had an affair. Yes, girl, can you believe it? I don't know why that girl won't leave those married men alone! It's hard enough trying to maintain a marriage without these single sisters going after our husbands like they're their own."

"It's so sad about Linda. She was diagnosed with cancer a year ago ... oh, her poor children ... *shh*, nobody's supposed to know. They want everyone to think those lumps in her breasts are benign. I wonder how she's doing. Hmm ... maybe she's getting pay-back for scandalizing the bishop's daughter."

"What do you think about that lady who comes to church every Sunday with those four kids? All she does is jump and dance in church. She's so distracting. Doesn't she know church is supposed to be a place of decency and order? If you ask me, that girl needs to chill and tend to disciplining that little boy of hers. Good grief!"

"One more thing: Cindy and Tracey are at it again over Trevor. When are those two going to get over the fact that he doesn't want either of them? Wait till he drops the bombshell that he's marrying Tiffany—those two girls are going to have a coronary when they hear that news. Serves them right. Trevor wants to move on, but they just will not let go. If you ask me, they need to get over their 'Trevor obsession.' But don't tell anyone, and if you do, you didn't hear a word from me."

Do any of the above scenarios sound familiar? When you hear similar words, do you think of the word *gossip*? Sadly, many church folk have heard so much gossip that they fail to recognize it for what it is. They lack the ability to "think outside this box" and see the hurting people behind the stories. Scandals have grown so common in the church that we've become desensitized to them.

When scandals come to light, we in the church tend to focus only on the sin, without looking at the events leading up to it. One reason we do this may be our own anxieties or fears of addressing issues that appear "vile," "disgraceful," or "immoral." Whatever the reason, we fail to get at the root of who the people involved in the scandal really are.

This is where "real talk" comes in. "Real talk" is important because it provides context, clarity, and tools to better resolve the issues in our lives. When confronted with an individual's failure, we should consider these questions before drawing any conclusions on the matter:

- What were the events leading up to the failure?
- What are we not hearing?
- Who hurt who and are there outstanding issues to resolve?

The answers to these questions can equip us to develop the whole person and to accomplish *proper* interventions so that hurting persons in our churches can be healed. Now let's look at the real testimonies concerning Minister Terry and the other church folk who were the subjects of the gossip above.

Minister Terry

Minister Terry is twenty-five years old. He got saved (gave his life to the Lord) in the church when he was twenty-three. Because he is the only member of his extended family who is in the church, the church plays a huge role in his life as a surrogate family.

Minister Terry has had a rough past. His mother is deceased and his father lives in another city. His parents divorced when he was only ten because, according to what he was told, his dad had an affair with Aunty Jane. His earliest recollections of his father are numerous fights concerning how he'd disgraced the family by "messing with Aunty Jane." Minister Terry's father eventually moved out, and Minister Terry hasn't had a strong relationship with him since. Once Terry became part of the church family, he especially cherished the relationship he had with his pastor, who made it a point to mentor him in the church.

During high school and college, Terry was known as a "player." He had numerous sexual experiences and left a long trail of broken hearts behind him. His last relationship before getting saved continued for eight months after Terry first gave his life to the Lord. His relationship with this young woman was serious, but he ended it abruptly, realizing he couldn't continue it now that he was in the church. There was no proper closure with the woman, even though Terry had contemplated marrying her one day.

He began to get more involved in the church and it became evident that the hand of the Lord was on his life. As soon as Terry took the microphone at church and spoke, people began hollering, crying, or standing. Obviously, Terry had a great gift. The church appreciated Terry and he moved quickly up the ranks. Within a year and a half, he was ordained as a minister.

Intense pressure to get married followed ordination. Under the guidance of his pastor (whom he highly respected), Minister Terry chose Lydia, a young woman who had grown up in the church and who seemed a perfect match. Minister Terry and Lydia wed after dating for seven months and now have a ten-month-old child.

During this period, another interesting event took place. Deacon Gregory's daughter gave her life to the Lord and now attends the same church as Minister Terry. She is the girl Terry had his last relationship with before getting saved—the girl he had contemplated marrying.

No one in the church knew their history.

Samantha

Samantha has a very dark past, but she is an extraordinary person. Her uncle sexually molested her from the time she was eight until she was eleven-years-old. Samantha has difficulty recalling most of her childhood. One vivid memory is that of an older boy raping her in high school. She cried for days and eventually gave her life to God. Unwilling to let her past stigmatize her future, she sought help.

The Sunday school class for new converts that Samantha attended had an awesome teacher who preached the Word of God and provided resources on how a Christian can grow in the Lord. After some time, Samantha felt very comfortable with her Sunday School teacher and started to open up to him. She told him not only about her uncle molesting her but also about the boy who had raped her at school. Samantha had an extraordinary ability to be open.

The Sunday School teacher, however, was overwhelmed by Samantha's openness and often did not know what to do with the information she shared. The more Samantha expressed herself to him, the more he felt out of control. He became so consumed by what Samantha told him that he developed insomnia, but he didn't want to let her down. He often found his mind racing rehearsing the details and traumatic experiences she shared like a rolling tape in a movie. He fought desperately to get it together.

Samantha did not let up. She continued to talk to him, seeking counsel and guidance on how to get through her pain. They spent hours talking on the phone, exchanging e-mails, texts, you name it, and over time a bond started to take shape. Eventually, her constant disclosures wore him out. He stopped fighting to keep out those images he formed in his mind and eventually just went with the flow.

In his time with her, he began to focus on the specifics of her sexual encounters and became more interested in these details than in helping her overcome her past. In fact, because he was under qualified to deal with Samantha's past and was not honest enough to acknowledge it and refer her to someone who could help her – this led to catastrophe. One day, Samantha broke down, saying she felt so lonely and that no one in her family was there to help her heal. Her Sunday school teacher embraced her and used his handkerchief to wipe her tears. From that point forward, everything changed. The boundaries had been breached and she now saw her Sunday School teacher in a different way.

Samantha expressed her appreciation to him for being there. Her father had left when she was only three and the Sunday School teacher was the only positive male figure in her life. She finally felt protected and although their initial interaction started innocently his mishandling of the situation, created an unhealthy dependency which became a type of seduction. Because Samantha had not yet worked through her response to the sexual aggression she'd experienced at a young age, she had a distorted sense of self. Her sexuality was the only power she thought she had and she used it to reward her Sunday school teacher for being there. So they had a sexual relationship, and what others called an affair was really a deep manipulation and abuse of power. Samantha now saw her Sunday school teacher as her soul mate and would not let go.

Meet Linda

Approximately eight years ago, Linda was working as an administrative assistant for her local church. Over time, Linda started to notice some invoices that were unaccounted for. Initially she let it go, thinking they were just mistakes, but she began to see a pattern developing, so she took it up with the board. At the same time this was happening, she had an altercation with the pastor's daughter. The pastor's daughter had wanted to participate as a volunteer in the church administration, but given that her dad was the pastor and some of the issues Linda was dealing with could potentially implicate him, she thought it unwise for the daughter to volunteer at that time for ethical reasons.

The daughter told her father that Linda had turned her down, and this created a difficult rift between Linda and the pastor. This happened at the same time she was approaching the board with the unsubstantiated invoices. The board dismissed her concern as frivolous and eventually decided that Linda was no longer a good fit. With little to no warning, it was announced to the church membership that Linda's term in the administrative role had expired.

Linda was devastated. She'd put her heart and soul into the church and was a long-standing member. The pastor's daughter was hired in her stead and Linda was humiliated to the core. She soon began to hear rumours of how she'd slandered the daughter's name out of jealousy. Linda was so broken and hurt that she became severely depressed. She still attended church but her motivation was gone. Nobody had ever come to her to ask what had happened and Linda felt like a leper.

About a year later, and no resolution to how she had been mistreated, Linda began noticing some small lumps under her arm. After they became severe, she went for a physical, and the doctor diagnosed benign cysts that could lead to cancer if she didn't get them removed. A major cause of cysts is stress.

Meet the woman with the four kids

This woman grew up in the church and got married at 21. Her husband left her when her fourth child was three months old. Some say he couldn't take the pressure, but who knows the real story here? Through all of this, the woman with the four kids never left the church, though she struggled immensely. Sometimes she had little food, and macaroni and cheese was a staple dinner for her family. Her week was incredibly stressful, with dropping off and picking up the kids at three different schools, and she had little time for herself. She trusted God. She believed that somehow and some way God would help her through it. Her faith was unrelenting.

Her third son had mild Attention Deficit Disorder (ADD). He had trouble focusing for long periods of time and became agitated easily. Despite the pressure from her son's school, she refused to medicate him, as she was well aware of the side effects of doing so. She knew of others who'd had undiagnosed ADD and led fruitful lives. She trusted God that her son would get better in time and she brought him to church in anticipation that he would be healed. The church was her escape and her release. When she was at church she didn't realize how boisterous her praise was, as she had no time to think about that. Her only concern was to give God her best, because she knew God would see her through. When she praised, she felt better and it gave her strength to face what would be another difficult week.

Meet Cindy and Tracey

Cindy and Tracey were roommates. They had known each other for 20 years and had lived literally like sisters. They had been in the church from their early teens; Cindy was now in her early 40s and Tracey in her late 30s. During their 20s, Cindy met a guy in the church whom she dated on and off. In fact, they never really dated as sweethearts do—their relationship was purely sexual with no strings attached. Cindy struggled with sleeping with him but thought he would one day marry her, so she held on. Her reasoning was *"Would he have stayed with me this long if he won't marry me?"* When asked by her roommate, Tracey, if they were going out, she always denied it, because she knew having sex with him was wrong and she didn't want to give Tracey any inkling of what was truly happening.

This constant denial eventually satisfied Tracey, especially after noticing that Trevor was coming on to her. She never felt she was betraying Cindy, because Cindy had told her they didn't have a relationship. After all, she really wanted someone in her life—her clock was ticking. She enjoyed the attention Trevor gave her, which gradually evolved into sweet words, flowers and soft touches. She remembers one day in particular when Trevor met her in the parking lot where she worked and offered her a ride home. That was when it happened. Trevor bought her ice cream, they walked in the park, and before you knew it, kissing turned to touching and touching turned to full-fledged sexual intercourse. As shocked as she was, it felt so good to get this attention. Tracey knew what she was doing was wrong, but she just wanted to be in the moment for a little while longer. That moment lasted for three years.

Neither Cindy nor Tracey knew what was happening until they began to hear rumblings in the church about how Trevor was playing both of them. They confronted each other about it, but they were so intertwined with Trevor and thought they were "the one" that they didn't believe each other and they turned on each other. Meanwhile, Trevor got tired of both of them and diverted his attention to a young virgin in a nearby church he thought he could settle down with. They planned to get married in a year. His fiancée told her best friend about their intentions. The fiancées best friend told her mother and she happened to be the usher at the church Cindy and Tracey attended. Everyone knew but poor Cindy and Tracey.

As dramatic as these stories may appear, they each get to the heart of the issue. By hearing the real talk, we see that the whisperings we initially heard lose steam. When it comes to matters of the heart, it must be dealt with delicately, in a non-judgemental way and with a lot of prayer. Broken hearts and sexual indiscretions cannot be dealt with overnight. It takes time, effort and skill. It requires acknowledgment, trust and motivation to reach true restoration. We can see in the respective cases of Samantha and Minister Terry that they both had unresolved issues from their past that trickled into the present. In the case of Terry, how often do we see people in our church who get saved and are married off before they can recite the 23rd Psalm? And then soon after, we see these same individuals intensely struggling with themselves and in their marriages, since they haven't been able to balance being a newborn babe in the Lord and the challenges that come with marriage. What are we afraid of? Why can't we stand by these new members and give them time to work through their pasts before we cast them in the same dark mould as others with similar struggles? Is that not the path to disaster?

Likewise, Cindy and Tracey were victims of deep manipulation by the same man. Because the two women were not honest with each other, they were left in a cloud of darkness that kept them away from the truth that was staring them in the face. Problem was, they couldn't hear the truth because no one directly *told* it to them. If the onlookers had thought of their daughters, sisters or close friends being in this situation, they would never have stood aside and watched these women make fools of themselves. But we indulge in these sorts of dramas for pleasure, somewhat like the way we indulge in a good cheesecake that will give us a bellyache by morning.

Another common issue in the church is character assassination. This is when we viciously attack individuals either purposely or unintentionally to destroy their reputation. To refer to the woman with the four unruly kids without a name dehumanizes her and attacks her ability as a mother. Little do we know, she cares deeply for her children; she uses the church as a place for her own healing and stress relief, as well as anticipating healing for her son. The conclusion made about her was based on false perceptions. Once we know her story, we would *want* to know her name and we would understand why she has "*a crazy praise*".

In the case of Linda, to suggest that a horrible disease is payback for alleged bad behaviour is to suggest that she deserves to suffer because she didn't handle the pastor's daughter right. In reality, Linda had great integrity as she sought for the truth and exposed the mishandling of God's money in the church. She was so severely wounded by being wrongfully attacked—without proper resolution and inquiry—that she internalized her hurts, which mutated into a serious physical disease. It's unfortunate, but many physical ailments that people in the church suffer are not genetic or just bad luck, but are directly caused by hidden pain, unresolved issues and character assassination. Next time we make a remark about someone's illness, let's think of Linda.

We in the church are being called to greater accountability in areas we've avoided for far too long. If we follow the life of Jesus, we see he had a very clear mandate, that is, to know the people that society does not want to know. He sought out the destitute, the unloved and the taken for granted. Through a gentle word or healing power, Jesus addressed the private pains of individuals by letting them know they mattered. He left a pattern for us to follow—for if we go after the gatekeepers in the church, imagine the possibilities of their reaching the world. He knew if we could convert the so-called vilest sinner, messed-up saint or obnoxious child, we could inevitably change the world. He knew the power of the *real* testimony and how it could affect pious living. This is what Jesus wants us to do—emancipate all church members so they are free to emancipate others. By learning about and understanding the private pains that exist for these people, we point others to Christ and remind them that nothing is too hard for God to work out.

But let's take a step back. What is it that the church is not getting? Or better, what is it that we may not understand about the church in the twenty-first century? If we ask this question differently, it is no longer just an indictment against the church but a challenge to understand the times. To better understand the church, then, we need to understand the age in which we live. As our society moves away from strong Christian values towards a more liberal sentiment, the role of the church is seen very differently.

In addition to its evangelical role, the central role of the church, particularly among the immigrant communities of the 1960s, was to facilitate the resettlement process of new immigrants. The church was like a governmental arm that offered social welfare for those in need. During this time, there was a very strong belief that the church should take care of the poor, destitute or vulnerable groups that needed a helping hand. This belief was based on Judaeo-Christian principles of community. The church, as part of its social justice mandate at the time built a strong social and cultural community to cater to the needs of its members.

However, as liberal values of individualism have become more pronounced over time and the age of seeking affluence has set in, we see people, particularly those who struggle economically, very differently. We see them as outcasts, worthless and responsible for their actions. This is a fundamental shift in how we perceive others and how we help those in need. The role of the church was to cater to the physical needs of its members (along with the spiritual, of course), and it has spent a lot of energy giving to and serving the community. The dynamic, however, is changing. The church is no longer giving handouts to help others but is now receiving handouts from its members, as things are much harder. Think about it.

Who provides the money offerings and helps to maintain and pay for the huge mortgages churches have accumulated? Who volunteers his or her time to do church business?

The answer, in part, lies in the pews. Perhaps churches cannot effectively address private indiscretions because their role has changed. They are no longer in the role of giver but of receiver—it is the pew members who keep them afloat. This is certainly not a conscious act, but I believe it plays out at the subconscious level. Preachers preach what people want to hear and we elevate persons who can give the church some prestige or even money. This was never the intent of the Gospel. Paul emphatically told Timothy to "preach the word; be instant in season, out of season; reprove, rebuke, exhort with all long-suffering and doctrine" (2 Timothy 4:2). Churches should be in the business of giving—the word, counsel, alms, love and rebuke.

The fear of tackling certain issues because of who may be behind them has much to do with the will to confront these issues. It also may have much to do with what the church may lose, so it is best to sweep things under the carpet and hope they will go away. We have all seen that some of the busiest people working in our church are often individuals with poor moral characters. The more we drift away from clear Christian biblical principles, the lower our will to address certain issues. Pew members have become so overburdened and overtaxed that they can hardly manage their own day-to-day affairs. When problems arise, without a dedicated prayer life, it becomes difficult to navigate their relationships with the church, and over time they can become depleted in spirit, mind and body. These are usually the junctures at which church people fall.

Who are pew members? you ask. They are the active church members who do not hold a position of authority, i.e., pastor, minister, elder or evangelist. More attention needs to be given to this very special group of people, as they are the pulse (philosophically speaking) of our church today. Pew members are those to whom we preach, with whom we plan our programs and to whom we go when the church needs help. Without them there is no church. Pew members have one of the most important functions in the church: they are the gatekeepers of knowledge. They have knowledge about the church and its members that the pastor will never possess. They help to create a parish community and are what makes attending church a worthwhile experience.

The church today has also become deeply political. It has obsessively focused on leadership to the detriment of the needs of pew members. We can always find a leadership conference or workshop on how to be a leader, but consider how little attention we pay to the faithful masses who make up our mega churches or our storefronts. We have made pew members virtually invisible as we strive to build hierarchical structures where only one person can be at the top. Certainly, we may have fulfilled our social mandate in meeting the physical and social needs of our members, but we've lost touch with those to whom we minister. Leaders no longer have their ears and eyes on the ground to understand the psychological and mental struggles of this time. Instead, the more church leaders amass financial fortunes and increase their personal security guards/armour bearers to keep people away from them, the more they get out of sync with the biblical principles of community.

People's ambition to gain riches in the church has given rise to immense anxiety and a sense of inadequacy if they fail. The rich preacher is held in very high esteem, even though half the single sisters in the church know him "personally." The pervasive indulgence in money, sex and infidelity are a demonic attack upon the church. How best to reframe and alter a church's purpose than to desecrate the temple where God should dwell? To make this work, all the enemy needs are overworked, devalued, detached pew members who are tired of the same ol' and the mess they see around them. It is no wonder why we have hit such a moral decline in our churches. The value we seek is in people and things, neither of which can bring true happiness in this life.

Our world has become a place where people can no longer be corrected. The gossip columns have trumped the reporting of world events like earthquakes, famines and pestilence, which are all markers of prophetic happenings that confirm the coming of the Lord. It is no coincidence that our news has become obsessed with the dirt about Hollywood stars. It is no coincidence that the church has followed suit, for we have been swept up in the tide of gossip about our brethren with little encouragement to uplift people who have fallen.

The church is a living and breathing entity that must maintain a clear distinction from the world. The church is God's habitation, which should endorse the importance of a strong spiritual family. He wants His people to assemble in His house as healthy citizens. Where boundaries have been breached, we need to repair them and equip our soldiers for the coming of the Lord. No longer do we want to be laced with problems that no one wants to deal with, as this undermines the power of the Gospel to change people's lives.

We don't want bloodied hands building our churches. King David recognized that he couldn't build a house of God because his hands had shed blood. His situation teaches us that there are consequences to our actions, and that this principle must be maintained to bring respect to the sacred institution that is the church. David testified to his limitations and he humbly passed the mantle to his son, Solomon. Today, what do we do? A married preacher sleeps with several pew members and we want to consecrate him as Bishop! This is not acceptable. It's no wonder the world looks at the church and doesn't want to be a part of it.

In this era of new technology and social networks, we cannot help but embrace the new ways of life. The church is feeling the impact of these changes and we have tried to keep up in order to appear relevant. The old folks will tell you that church is not what it used to be. As grumpy as they may sound, they are on to something. They reminisce about how the choir used to sing, how people used to pray, how dedicated pastors used to be and how close a walk with God people had. Now, as churches move from one generation to the next, they are not valued in the same way. The old folks may not have articulated it in this manner, but they are correct in saying that change is happening at an alarming rate. For example, consider the declining choir ministry. Church choirs, which once had up to a hundred members in the 1990s and which promoted strong community bonding amongst the pew, have been replaced in the millennium with praise team ministries that have four or five members. Is anyone taking note of this travesty? Because of the way it's structured, the praise team cannot accommodate large numbers and this new area of ministry has become more individualized. There is certainly no problem with having a praise team ministry, but we should have something to involve the large number of people who have been displaced. In some churches, the praise team ministry has obliterated the ministry of the choir, and we wonder why we, particularly our youth, have become so disconnected.

As another example, one not short on controversy, the vintage hymnal is no longer in many churches today. God bless the few churches who continue to sing the hymns whereby the young persons in the church can understand the distinction of the historical sacred songs from the contemporary. The sharing of the hymnal with the person who sits next to us in the pew has now been replaced by a power point projector that displays contemporary songs in which, at times, only the praise leaders are well versed. As the hymnal has been removed and the pew member no longer brings their bible with them to church since our songs and scripture verses are splattered on screens, the sacredness of community fellowship is lost. Pew members are so disconnected with one another and what is going on around them that they have become desensitized to their surroundings. People now stare into space to catch the words and watch the performance.

This may sound extreme, but the point I am making is that the pew member is no longer invested in the same way. Technology is a necessary tool to push the Gospel, but we also must be very careful about the way it ruptures the community idealism once found in the church. The rapidity of change must be balanced with why we sing the way we do, preach the way we do and organize the way we do. Things are getting harder. The family is breaking apart. The community is under siege. Change is inevitable, but the change we are experiencing has resulted in the annihilation of a community that once centered on the pew.

We need to purposely maintain things that promote fellowship and community in order to attract a generation who thinks they can make it on their own. The practice of feet washing for communion/the Lord's Supper may be deemed irrelevant in the modern church, but it is an example of the way the church promotes community. Besides following the biblical instruction, the practice teaches us many things. To stoop to the menial task of washing another person's feet is to demonstrate the spirit of love, equality and brotherhood within the church family. It also aims to teach the importance of service in our lives. The act of feet washing is taken from the biblical passage (John 13:4, 5) where Jesus washed the feet of his disciples during the Passover. The implication of this passage is to show that everyone is equal in the sight of God; therefore, to refuse to follow the example of Jesus is to exalt oneself above him and to live in pride. Although foot washing is not practised in many religions, the literal interpretation of this act can provide a constant reminder that all are equal before God from the pulpit to the pew. There are things we should preserve. Perhaps there are other things in our local church that once promoted community belonging that need to be revived. Consider them and fight to keep them alive.

The critique against technology is not to resist the fervour for excellence but to be critical of our appetite to do things quickly that creates the erosion of the community and social centrality that was once found in the church. This is important because the sense of disconnection and individualism we experience in the church is hampering the way we deal with problems. If I don't feel connected to my brother or sister that sits with me in the pew, the silent pain that is experienced forever remains silent. We need to recognize the church as a God-ordained institution that is able to meet the great challenges of today. There is a pew member who arrives on Sunday and is crying, then leaves depressed for the remainder of the week. There is a battered woman who attends church with suicidal thoughts as she wonders if there is anything worth living for. There is a man who is struggling because he is having an affair and is finding it difficult to break free. This struggle can continue for weeks, months and even years.

In the case of a woman who is struggling in her marriage, it becomes obvious to her child that everything is not okay. That child sees Mommy happily singing in the choir and helping with church administration, but also sees Mommy crying during the week when she's subjected to the abuse from Daddy. Such contradictory displays of emotion can create a profound sense of inauthenticity in our children, and over time such children lose respect for the house of God. This generation is not like the former. They will speak to what doesn't make sense for them and not play along. If our children grow up in this environment and don't see authenticity in the church, we are in danger of raising a generation that will not respect the God of their fathers. If you fast-track the little girl who asks, "Why is Mommy so happy on Sunday mornings at church but the rest of the week she's talking about leaving Daddy and taking us far away?" in fifteen years, you will see that this now grown-up child has learned to conduct herself in the same way.

Consider if you were the pew member who wonders when something will be done about Rob, who you've been sleeping with for four months but who gets to preach every other month. This can't be okay, you say, and the guilt is killing you. You watch Rob come to church with his family every Sunday, but by Tuesday he's in your arms, inside of you, cradling you with the unspoken hope that you can be together. But this can't be right, you say again. You want him but can't have him! Someone needs to know, but you can't tell, for what would they think of you? Why isn't anyone hearing you scream? You sit here in the pew, but you see so much and you're hurting. You want to stop, but how can you? You're too deeply in love.

Or consider your plight if you were a young pew member who sits in church and wonders why the Mother of the church is talking about how awful young Lydia is dressing when her own daughter is the schoolyard whore. You see her daughter every day at school, but because of who she is, she never gets the negative attention poorly dressed Lydia gets. Why do we favour some people and reject others?

And then there is Freddie. He directs the choir, runs the praise team and facilitates workshops, but the whole world knows he's struggling with his sexuality. We pew members act as if we don't see it and shove every single sister his way in hopes that she will beat this lifestyle tendency out of Freddie. But don't rock the boat too hard, because we can't wait to see Freddy on Sunday mornings—no one can do praise and worship like him! But in the back of our minds we wonder who is going to minister to Freddy. Who is going to ask Freddy those hard questions if in fact he does need help?

Let us not forget the pocket-with-holes church ministry. The more money you give, the less you have, contrary to what the prayer line promised you. You still don't have your new car and five-bedroom house. What you have is debt and a lot of it. The church asked for a sacrificial offering again—there were three offerings in one service—and you sacrificed paying your household bills to contribute to the "special offering," which doesn't seem special anymore because they ask for it every Sunday. The more you give, the more they ask. Something has got to be wrong with the church finances, you say. You want to stop tithing because you can barely make ends meet, but you know you will be doomed to hell. No doubt there will be a Sunday morning sermon entitled "Tithe or You're Doomed."

And finally, there is humble Helen, another pew member we've all seen. She has been in the church from when her eyes were at her knees. She sits in the same spot every Sunday. What a patient, faithful and willing pew member she is. But did you know that Helen is so depressed that she cries herself to sleep? That she feels too much pressure on her to be the goody-goody and the go-to person? Did you know that humble Helen thinks she has a disease but actually is physically okay? Her mind has been so plagued with dying and the notion that the devil is going to hurt her that she is too scared to go to a doctor.

Poor Helen can't break the darkness that circles in her mind because she is too busy helping people. Nobody knows that she feels life has passed her by. She rejected seven marriage proposals in her lifetime, all because none of the men were good enough for her pastor. She has no children, no spouse, and little family except the church. People glance at Helen and say, "Oh, I wish I could be like her." Helen has to play along, she has to be obedient and help others, or everything will fall apart.

That is church life. As harsh as this may seem, these are just reflections on the many deep issues pew members experience and observe. We see people crying at the altar not only because of their gratitude for the atoning blood of Jesus but often because of profound emotional circumstances that are robbing them of life. The need to tend to these wounds is now. Only a spiritual encounter can break the shackles so many in the church bear. We need God's infinite power.

From the pulpit to the pew, the silent cries are testifying. The church has done a great job feeding and teaching people the word of God, but it must be called into greater accountability to address the whole man or woman. The gathering of people on a voluntary basis cannot be taken for granted. Regardless of the wheat and the tares, the hypocrites and the genuine, or the righteous and the filthy, people need a place to come that gives them hope. They also need to come to a place where they can be real.

This chapter may appear harsh and an attack on the church, but it simply aims to expose the mess so we can collectively clean it up. You may be able to relate in whole or in part to issues that have been mentioned. You may be stressed out by some of the content on these pages, as it appears there is so much to tackle. Let us be clear: what is church life you ask? Many would say it is life itself. It is our day-to-day encounters, struggles, weaknesses and strengths. It is our meeting place and our community, which brings closeness for individuals who desire to be in the presence of the Lord. It is a family that is responsible for ensuring its members are properly fed, nurtured and loved. The paradox of the church is that despite the silent cries behind closed doors, it is a place people come to worship a God who makes sense to them. Many criticize the church for not handling issues, but the church should be the place to handle real issues for people who refuse to let go of their faith.

Some chapters may speak to you more than others, but rest assured the content will look at issues church folk deal with and provide solutions to hidden secrets so people can be real. What's in darkness must come to light so God's people can be free. This book is about the private and painful episodes in life and making them public so you can be healed through the power of God. Not all of us will be able to consult a counsellor to sort through pain, but generally speaking, everyone can read. I pray that the words on these pages will minister to you directly so that you and your God can work it out. As you read, you may uncover those secrets that hold you down. If this happens, tell God all about it and if necessary, pray that He leads you to ongoing deliverance and healing. Church life is awesome, but God is calling us to find balance. The Sunday morning performance doesn't work anymore in an age of depression, financial crisis and family breakdown. That is real talk. You don't have to act anymore. You can be changed, delivered and set free. Just read on and you will see how.

And the LORD turned the captivity of Job, when he prayed for his friends: also the LORD gave Job twice as much as he had before.
(Job 42:10 KJV)

Chapter 3

Friends, a Gift from God

So now that we have gotten all that real talk out in the open, let's get to the heart of the matter: you. Let's turn the light inward and recognize one of the important things that we sometimes take for granted: friends. This chapter is about appreciating those whom God has placed in your life and reflecting on friendships that serve a specific purpose.

In all of your experiences, there are usually a small number of people who have journeyed with you during tumultuous times. Mark those people who gave you a smile, a nudge or a shoulder to cry on. Like flowers in a garden, they serve a particular purpose, which is for you to grow into what God wants you to be.

Consider the tulip and how it grows in the cold and snowy winter. It usually blooms in early spring in anticipation of summer weather. Tulips are encouragers of a brighter season despite the winter-like conditions in which they grow. When we see tulips begin to bloom, it tells us that something new is on the horizon. These flowers bring hope that the season is about to pass and the sun is soon to shine. When summer finally comes, the tulips are nowhere in sight. They have fulfilled their call until the next spring season, and the torch is passed to the flowers that bring beauty during the summer.

I use the analogy of the tulip to help us understand the nature of friendships and the role we play in one another's lives. Healthy relationships are essential components to living whole and productive lives. There are certain friends who will show up when we need them most. At other times we may never hear from them, but they are near us nevertheless. Just as seasons change, so do our relationships, and there will be times when you will face things on your own. One of the biggest mistakes we make is assuming that when we go through difficult times, no one cares. We wonder why no one is calling, why no one is asking for us and why everyone seems to be pulling away. We may interpret this distance negatively and fail to understand that some people just don't know what to say. Often the distance we feel from others is really our own distance as we attempt to sort out what we're going through. But if you were a fly on their wall, you would see them praying and crying for you, just waiting for your storm to pass. We may never hear those prayers or be witness to them, but we must believe that they do help to pull us through.

If we are honest with ourselves, we would admit that when we face certain trials, we do not see things clearly, and this affects the way we interact with people. We tend to internalize our problems and draw away from people before properly assessing our course of action. Your friends may not be talking to you in the way they used to because your body language is telling them that something is off. You have to understand that not everyone will tune into your pain and not everyone will understand how to deal with it. Many prefer to respect your privacy and not to get involved, but behind closed doors they are praying for you.

One of the main strategies of the enemy is to isolate you from other people just enough so that you can be part of his master plan. Your feelings of withdrawal are aimed to isolate you and feed mistrust into your spirit so that you think you can make it on your own. Pulling away gives room for the enemy to wreak havoc on a weakened vessel. I have seen time and time again that when people go through certain trials, they feel the need to abruptly abandon their friendships. It is interesting that these feelings seem to crop up, not when we are on the mountaintop, but when we are in the valley. This is a deliberate plan of the enemy. You may think that things are clear in your mind when you feel the need to put friendships on hold or possibly terminate them. But what you don't realize is that you may leave a trail of broken hearts behind you, as these friends are wounded by your sudden unexplained actions.

The time when you are going through trials is never a good one to make drastic changes in your life. This is because your judgment may be impaired while you are preoccupied with sorting through your turmoil. It is best to wait until the dust settles so that you can use wisdom to carefully and sensitively deal with your relationships. In every situation, always seek to find out what God is teaching you, and don't jump to conclusions.

Good friendships are important in our individualistic age—they help prevent the shipwrecked mentality plaguing the minds of many people. A shipwrecked mentality is what I call the "castaway spirit," which is a spirit of the enemy that is pushed into the minds of believers that makes them feel rejected, discarded or thrown away. They feel that there is no hope or trust that can be fostered in the individualistic island that the enemy has created, and so the castaway creates his or her own world and means of coping. The moment hope is lost is the moment the castaway accepts his or her fate.

If you recall the 1960s television show *Gilligan's Island,* there were seven passengers that were shipwrecked on a deserted island as a result of a storm. Every episode focused on their plan to escape the island, a plan that was usually foiled by Gilligan's clumsy and coincidental interference. We may have fond memories of Gilligan in terms of the humour he gave us, but if considered at a spiritual level, his actions represent the interference the enemy exerts to spoil any attempt to rescue ourselves from our predicaments. We may have become burdened by the hopelessness of a shipwrecked life, but we must have faith that someone will throw us an anchor or spot our smoke signal and help us get off that island. It may be a cliché, but everybody needs somebody in this Christian race. So be careful of ending friendships in haste and be courageous in starting new ones in faith.

The way we deal with adverse situations varies from one person to the next. Some people are very open about their struggles and have no problem discussing them. The culture of the church, however, is quite different. Because we have become so accustomed to spiritualizing daily living and dealing with fallen members in a militaristic and judgmental way, we are left with little room to be open. Consequently, people withdraw for fear of being treated harshly. In the church we distance ourselves by building walls, because that is the easiest thing to do in settings where confidentiality is the foremost concern. Being very conscious of how we handle people in the church, we must seek to break down these walls. The way we talk to people has a lot to do with how those who are hurting will cope with their circumstances. As Proverbs 15:1 tells us, "A soft answer turneth away wrath: but grievous words stir up anger." A soft word can defuse a hostile situation. Let us think before we speak and ponder the result we wish to achieve.

A misconception we have in the church is that when we go through trials that are caused by sin, nobody will know. Regardless of your secret and how tightly held it is, you cannot hide from the presence of the Lord. While it is true that nobody may come up to you and discuss the specifics of your situation, God has a way of alerting you so that you can face the reality of your error. So regardless of the state you may be in, it is dangerous to isolate yourself from an arena where God can get your attention. When urgings come at you to stop attending church, this is the time when you push. The church service you do not want to attend could be the one when you hear a sermon that speaks directly to your circumstances, or it could be the day when those faithful few encourage you to get back on track.

When the prophet Nathan approached King David about his sin with Bathsheba, he did not specifically say what David had done. Instead, he told David a parable about the unjust treatment of another man. Nathan applied wisdom and knew that this approach was inspired by God and would alert David to his sin. Good relationships teach us how to approach one another when things are not going well. They teach us to weigh our words and encourage us to seek the will of God and his timing in what to say and when to say. We have all heard that it is not *what* we say but *how* we say it that determines the response we will get. The way Nathan confronted David was an unquestionable rebuke, but it still got the result God wanted. David surrendered his will to God, repented of his sin and became one of the greatest kings of Israel that ever lived. David was a man after God's own heart (Acts 13:22). The Bible doesn't tell us if David acknowledged his sin in private prior to meeting with Nathan, but there are certain situations that require exposure, openness and direct contact with God.

What we struggle with in the church is our approach to dealing with weakened vessels. We like to sweep things under the carpet to avoid the pain of working through sin. We also tend to avoid certain topics because we do not have the appropriate skills or expertise to deal with them. Good relationships will teach us how to get to the bottom of issues in order to bring forth true restoration. We cannot afford to sweep sin under the carpet because we are afraid of the repercussions. If sin is not dealt with, it festers like cancerous cells that will one day make a fatal appearance. Because situations have not been properly addressed within the church, these appearances manifest themselves as public scandals that cause it to lose credibility.

The hypocrisy of those who commit sin but feel they don't have to *deal* with sin becomes a stench to those it affects. The sense of injustice that people feel when issues are mishandled can have a profound impact on how they manage the situation. We have seen that the ways some individuals cope when they are directly affected by another's misdemeanour can turn them into whistle blowers outside the walls of the church. They may resort to calling the media or the police in order to bring some attention and resolution to the issue. Others may draw into their shells or become severely disillusioned with their lives and the church. We need some Nathans who are not afraid to deal with people and their problems. Our lack of Nathans is shown by our inability to accept the outcome of our confrontation with sin. We need the fortitude, courage and will to stand up against the wrong. We don't stand up because we fear being jeered at, mocked and scorned, and we hold those fears because our characters have been bruised somewhere in our Christian journey. Nathan stood up for God, and although he confronted David, he didn't leave him alone. In 1 Kings Chapter 1, we are shown that Nathan continued to be David's prophetic advisor until David was old and sickly. He was a witness to the successful battles that David won throughout his life. David's future was greater than his past, and at the end of David's life, Nathan continued to be there for him, offering strategic counsel and wisdom. We need relationships that keep us accountable and mindful of the call of God in our lives.

The Nathan- and-David account provides a good pattern for us to follow in terms of how God will get our attention to do what is right. We must entreat each other to address the failures in our lives through wisdom, knowledge and understanding. The way we deal with God's precious people should be to help them reach their destiny. We cannot afford to make mistakes in how we handle people's lives, for destiny has an appointment with them in years to come. We may preach against sin, but some may still fall. But if they fall, we've got to catch them and not leave them on their own.

We cannot change people—only God can do that. Change comes about when there are relational and conclusive reasons to alter our behaviour. We should always seek to build up the fallen and support them until God gets their attention. If you are struggling and a friend is not there to help pull you out, remember this one thing: like King David, you can have a future greater than your past! Our job is to be open vessels and have mature characters so that God can use us as vehicles to get His job done.

In another biblical example, Adam tried to hide from his sin. When he disobeyed and ate of the Tree of Knowledge, he pulled away and covered himself with fig leaves, as his eyes had been suddenly opened to a world he previously had not seen. His nakedness represented shame, and his attempt to cover it up was outside the norm of what he usually did in the Garden. Likewise, you will observe at times that you will do drastic things that are outside the norm. You may get a tattoo, drastically cut your hair or lose weight quickly, all of which are often indicators of an attempt to cover up or purge yourself of a particularly trying situation. For Adam, it was just a matter of time before God asked him the important question, "Where art thou?" That question is pivotal to us today. The human urge to hide when we do wrong because we feel shame is nothing new. Our tendency to pull away from people and hide beneath other types of covering can be related to what occurred in the Garden of Eden. We may use a pulpit, a pew, a job, an addiction or a marriage as a cover. The question, "Where art thou?" is one you may have to confront. This question may come years after a trauma, test or disappointment, but if you do not deal with it now, it will deal with you. *Where art thou?*

We must purposely pursue and maintain good and healthy relationships. We also cannot conclude that every trial someone faces is the result of sin. Job's friends could not withstand the pressure he was experiencing and so could not help him in his process. They saw Job's condition as a result of something he must have done and preferred to withdraw rather than help him to weather his storm. Some people have dealt with terrible childhood traumas that resurface in adulthood. You may find that at certain junctures of your life, tensions are created, and people around them will not understand their behaviours. But instead of blaming or mocking them, we need to be intuitive enough to understand that their behaviours may be the result of something we do not understand.

Job's tests (albeit not related to his childhood) in principle show us that some friends will not understand the pull of God in your life. Nor will they always understand why you act the way you do. They may blame you for your predicament—but do not allow that to make you bitter. You know what is what, and where God wants you to go, and you can't take others with you. It does not mean these friends are bad; it could mean that God has a path that only you can take.

Job's friends misinterpreted what he was going through, and they are like many in the church today. When we see people struggling, as discussed in Chapter 2, we do not know their story. If the friends of Job had talked *to* him rather than talked *at* him, they might have arrived at a different conclusion. When you are being attacked for things that are based on ill perceptions, don't worry. These situations can push you in God's direction, where you can begin to question the negative influences in your life and refocus on the things of God.

In any relationship we enter, it is important that God is first. He is the only one who can keep us on track when things go wrong. If you learn what has happened to someone before he or she falls, you will see that the fall is often preceded by a bitter relationship or a difficult winter, things that can bring him or her low. This is why we must be properly insulated in our winter seasons by warm and compassionate individuals who can provide spiritual nurturing.

I remember a dark period in my life when I was on the verge of throwing in the towel. The pressure was too burdensome, and the pain I had from a broken relationship was too great. I had no strength to carry on. In a last-chance attempt to see if God was with me, I asked a friend at the time the question, "Have you ever felt like giving up?" The friend did not know the darkness I was experiencing—or maybe she did. In paraphrase, she responded, "No, I Love God too much and cannot let him down!" That response immediately cut into the darkness I was experiencing and gave me a glimmer of hope. If that friend had lamented with me and validated my negative feelings, I believe that would have been a major push toward my destruction. I needed a friend to lift me and encourage me, and to give me a positive word, not to join me in my pain. Moments like that I will never forget. That was one of my rock-bottom experiences and a reminder that spiritual friends have a purpose in everyone's lives. This is why I appreciate and value friends in our Christian walk. They are conduits of God's word and can be propagators of life.

Building friendships and relationships is about communication and trust. It takes a mature individual to speak about feelings, whether good or bad, and address them as they come. If each of us could have predicted unhappy events in our lives, we certainly would have taken a detour. But as Romans 8:28 (KJV) says, "…we know that all things work together for good to them that love God, to them who are the called according to His purpose." Even in the worst situation, good can come out of it.

If you do not have good relationships, seek to establish a circle of friends who are spiritually grounded. If you're in a situation where friends are causing you misery and grief, you need to bring them to God and ask what their purpose is for your life. It would be easier if God just told us that "your lesson this year is not to keep malice," but things don't work that way. God will take us on long and short journeys, many of which we have to repeat until we *get* the lesson He is trying to teach us. If you have good relationships, try to cherish them and strengthen them in God. If a relationship seems strained or just doesn't feel right, don't jump to conclusions. Use prayer to seek direction about why you feel that things aren't right. At the perfect time you can give the friend a phone call and do some real talk. This approach is sure to break up the enemy's plan, and the outcome will be better than what it was before.

It is interesting that the same people you think you do not need end up being the very people you *will* need one day. So in this Christian race, strive to be good, think good and talk good, for life has a way of turning things around. This is why we must be so careful in our attempts to sever relationships we think we do not want. Life is a full circle designed for you to mature to the level that God wants you to go.

I can remember asking God to remove someone from my life because that someone had hurt me. I prayed and challenged Him to take this person out of my heart and out of my life (not by death, of course). In my pain, I couldn't understand why I didn't get the release I wanted. As I repeatedly made my ignorant request in my prayer closet to remove the impact this person had had on me, the result was usually a prayer of intercession for that friend. When I wanted to confront this friend on several occasions in anger, God expressly told me no. He always pulled me away.

It took me a year of praying through this before being reconciled with my friend and understanding that this person was divinely placed in my life to help birth this book. What I had thought was done or said was different than what came to light. Imagine how different my life would be if I had not had that experience and listened to the voice of God. My destiny would have been altered and my call to be a kingdom writer would have been thwarted. Never did I imagine the manifestation of God's blessings in my life that would come just by holding on and not doing what I wanted to do. I share this to say that if you decide to walk away from a friendship, make sure you talk it over with the Lord with much prayer and honesty. The way you think things should be done may not be according to God's will. He sees our future and knows the path we have to take.

This experience taught me the power of praying through pain! It taught me the importance of discipline, perseverance and constantly asking God to purge the negativity that prevented me from making the right decision. Praying through pain gave me a deeper appreciation of prayer. You will find that when you pray through pain, these prayers don't focus on you, but on the glory of God that leads you to pray for others who may be the object of your hurt. You will find yourself at a place of worship that doesn't make sense in your current state of affairs. You will cry out your hurt from the depth of your soul, but you will go where your physical body cannot take you.

Praying through pain is a purging process. It can reveal the real you and the purposes God will birth in your life. A prayer through pain takes courage and enormous surrender. These are the prayers God wants us to get to. Your pain can birth your destiny to pursue. Don't point fingers, but get on your knees and pray! Pray through your pain, pray through your trauma and pray through your failures. That is where God wants you. In praying through your pain, seek discipline in your walk with the Lord, since discipline is an important attribute for any Christian. As you endure the circumstances you have to face, keep your ears trained to heaven to hear from God. Paul reminds us in 2 Timothy 2:3 (KJV) that we should "endure hardness as a good soldier of Jesus Christ." It will never be easy, but a relationship with God comes from truth from the inward parts (Psalms 51, KJV). No pain, no gain! God knows the true you, so demonstrate who you are and gain your victory.

Don't be afraid to call someone a friend. Good spiritual friends will be there when you pass through your storm and they will be patient with you until it ends. We refer to members of the church family as brothers and sisters, but in some circumstances this protocol tends to be a way to avoid calling someone a friend, since doing so has a lasting impact on him or her. Calling someone a friend creates a sense of responsibility, accountability and vulnerability. It is not so easy to walk away from people you have a history with and have learned to appreciate.

If we refrain from friendships or have a hard time holding on to them, we may be holding on to past hurts from friends that make us steer away from being put in that vulnerable situation again. If you find it difficult to call someone a friend, it could mean that there is some unresolved issue in your life you need to deal with. Conflict, which everyone naturally encounters, helps us to mature from infancy to childhood and from adolescence to adulthood. Conflict teaches us perseverance, openness, maturity, patience and strength to resolve difficult circumstances. If you run from conflict, you are running from developing your maturity in God, and you must challenge yourself to grow in ways that are outside your comfort zone.

Friends may be risky to have but so is buying a house. If you are paralyzed by the risk of purchasing a new house, you will be a renter for the rest of your life and you will never experience the satisfaction of being an investor who owns a home. There are bills to pay, renovations to make and payments that might get tight at times, but you would not sell your house because of these challenges. Similarly, unless you take risks in having friendships and understand the good they can provide, you will miss out on great opportunities for growth that can take you to a higher level in God. Don't allow things to fester in your spirit. It's best to nip them in the bud and not let the root of bitterness grow. The more you do that, the easier it becomes to move through conflicts and appreciate friends in a deeper way.

Beware of opposite sex friendship attractions. Keep your friendships pure and clean. We need to know the difference between positive and negative friends. Not everyone is evil and not everyone will betray you, but be discerning of wolves in sheep's clothing. Keep focused on who the real adversary is, for he is not your friend. Being a negative friend does not necessarily mean that the person is bad, but rather, that his influence on your life is bad.

Try not to align yourself with people who make you do things and go places you know you shouldn't. Friends for whom you *have* crossed the line, for example, with whom you've become sexually involved, should be shunned strongly, for these friendships cannot go back to what they were. Don't kid yourself. If you have breached your friendship in this manner, turn the other way and acknowledge your mistake.

In the church, it is unhealthy to maintain a relationship where sexual encounters once took place as if the history were erased from your memory. Don't ignore the facts. We all know someone we can go to if we want to party, be illicit and not be challenged about our destructive course of action. We also know individuals who will pray with us and tell us the truth whether we like it or not. If you sleep with a person and you are calling that person a friend and you see them every week in the pew, you are looking for trouble. For the Christian it will always be a constant reminder of where you've been and where you can go again, so boundaries must be properly drawn and distance enforced in these circumstances. This is a breached friendship that must be purged, disassociated with and acknowledged for what it is.

A healthy friendship should not be one-sided. You should not be the only one who gives of your time and emotions and does not receive anything positive in return. (By a positive return, I do not mean money, information or access to something you want. That is not friendship, but more like a business transaction.) Friendships should involve mutual respect, and if your relationship lacks this, you should seriously question the authenticity of that relationship and why you are in it. If you feel a sense of emptiness and emotional decay after being with certain individuals, they may not be the best people to have in your inner circle. They are like leeches that suck the blood out of you until you're depleted of your resources, which you were supposed to plant in fertile ground. But if the people around you inspire and motivate you, they are exactly the individuals you want in your inner circle. Pour into them, invest into them, and you will get favourable results.

Finding and keeping reciprocal friendships is especially important for leaders in the church, who give their time and physical presence to others. They, too, need friends from whom they receive encouragement or a spiritual word from time to time. Even in our political structures, perhaps especially in our political structures, the prime minister or president needs an inner circle of people he calls friends. This person needs their encouragement and support, in order to deal with the nation's affairs when things get challenging. Without this environment of friends and advisors, leaders can become suspicious of who is around them, and this insecurity and lack of trust can affect their decision-making. Presidents, prime ministers and preachers need informed opinions. They need insight, and they need to hear it from those who know the pulse of the people. These people have to be carefully picked, spiritual and they're usually those with a long history and proven loyalties, who can be trusted to tell the truth for the interests of a greater good.

Be truthful to yourself and strive to build strong friendships. Pick up the courage and reconcile yourself to a friend. Send an e-mail and put out a positive word. Send a text and appreciate someone today. You will find that you will see the preciousness of God's people and not respond negatively as others pass through the ups and downs of life. Be the friend who provides support to someone going through hard times. That loan will be repaid to you one day as you pass through your own storms.

Whatever your current circumstances, friends are a gift from God. I encourage you to seek to build spiritual relationships and to appreciate the importance of friendships that are inspired by God. Friends help keep you accountable and protected, and they may be placed in your life to teach you something and bring out the best in you.

Contrary to what you may have been told or to what you may believe, there will be someone when you need him/her. Value everyone and pray for everyone! Learn to appreciate the unique roles that people play. Your prayer partner may be there to encourage your prayer, but he or she may have no place in other areas of your life. That friend at school can give you information on obtaining your first mortgage and never give his/her life to God, but is a friend nevertheless. Friends may fade in and fade out of your life, but they can open your eyes to things. See who is around you and know why they are there. Use wisdom and appreciate those flowers that bloom in your season. Flowers fade as seasons change, but friends are flowers in God's garden awaiting their next season to bring beauty into someone's life. Those flowers may not bloom in your season, but they are there to fulfill another purpose. May you find good friends and appreciate who is around you. They are a gift from God.

*O my God, I am too ashamed and disgraced
to lift up my face to you, my God, because our
sins are higher than our heads and our guilt has
reached to the heavens.
(Ezra 9:6 NIV)*

Chapter 4

Guilty Stains

There are memories that linger in our minds and bring warmth and pride for the great things we have accomplished in this life. But just as these great memories live on, so do the traumatic ones that are caged behind darkened cells of guilt, shame and trauma. These dark memories that seem to never let you go are called guilty stains that won't wash out. This chapter is about addressing the stains of a bad decision, childhood trauma or whatever secret struggle a pew member contends with. The guilty stains that come in the forms of regret, embarrassment and deep pain are what we want to expose. We will learn about the guilt's we carry, their purpose and how we can best overcome them. We will also delve into understanding the enemy's plan to polish your guilty stains so that you are left in a state of hopelessness. You may have been struggling for a long time, but you are not alone. Thank God that He has the answer to every debilitating struggle and memory that may have kept you bound for far too long.

The things you have gone through, no doubt, have sometimes been challenging, and you may wonder why you are still here and how you are still living. If you find yourself thinking more about the negatives of your yesterday than your today, you may have some guilty stains to deal with. As William Cowper's ol' hymn declares:

> There is a fountain filled with blood,
> Drawn from Immanuel's veins,

> And sinners plunged beneath that flood
> Lose all their guilty stains.

As this hymn reminds us, God brings hope that your guilty stains will be removed. It is important that you understand that no matter what you have passed through in this life, all power is possessed by Christ our King, and he says that no weapon (of guilt) that is formed against you will prosper (Isaiah 54:17). You can live in victory regardless of your past traumas and bad mistakes. All it takes is a made-up mind that you will no longer live in yesterday because tomorrow is too bright.

Guilt is one of the hardest emotions to deal with. We feel it as early as infancy once we learn the difference between right and wrong. A child who steals a cookie, then quickly confesses, does so because his guilt tells him he has done something wrong. Somewhere along the way, a parent told that child he shouldn't steal and shouldn't lie. The child understands that this is a truth he must accept, and as a result, he forms a moral code by which to live. The way we deal with guilt as adults, then, has much to do with the way we have been socialized and the moral code, or standard, we've been shown.

Guilt is a cognitive and emotional experience that tells us that we have violated this moral code, which may have come from our legal system, as well as from our religious persuasion or family culture. Like a compass, our moral standards serve as roadmaps to put us on track for doing the right thing. As Christians, the moral code we follow is the word of God, which teaches the importance and the relevance of repentance. The act of repentance is a choice we make to change our mind and turn to God. Repentance is a confession for violating God's biblical mandate, and this should be an undisputed belief. When we do wrong, we should be sorry and we should act upon that sorrow to make things right.

If we violate the moral code that has been set for us, guilt will kick in like an alarm bell. This alarm bell of guilt does not turn off by itself. It takes action and diligence by the person to get back in line with God. You may be able to drown the alarm bell of inner guilt by doing other things, but the time will come when the annoyance of that sound will trigger unhappiness in your life and tell you that something needs to be corrected.

When violations of a moral code are unresolved, the resulting guilty stains put stress on your mind and body. This stress can manifest itself in unhealthy behaviours. For example, a woman who was abused as a child and believes it was her fault may internalize this trauma by having illicit sexual encounters. Or, she may become reclusive or even develop suicidal thoughts. Another adult with an abusive childhood may turn to such compulsive behaviours as excessive washing or bathing to rid herself of the unclean feeling of the assaults, or may punish the body by overeating, starving or mutilating it in some way. Others simply may file their traumatic experiences away, as you do with documents in a filing cabinet. All these behaviours and more are examples of coping mechanisms used to numb the effects of guilt on the mind. If these negative behaviours are not tackled, the trauma a person has experienced can become a stain on her mind, like pure grape juice splattered on white clothing. No matter how much detergent is used on that stain, it will not go away until you perform the more drastic measure of applying disinfectant bleach.

Shame is a very painful emotion that works together with guilt. Shame and guilt are not the same thing. Guilt is a stabilizer to keep you in line with your moral compass. Shame, on the other hand, has to do with your self-perception when bad things happen to you. It comes when you punish yourself for these bad things. Shame may make you feel that you are defective, awful and useless, and you may want to go away, disappear or even die. The embarrassment and disgrace of traumatic experiences can suck you dry, and make you believe you are undeserving of success and happiness. For example, a parent's extramarital affair that has gone public can bring shame for the child, even though the child had nothing to do with it. But because that child is related to that family member, the public perception of the child may be negative as well. Children can become defined by the actions of their parents, as if to say they will follow the same paths. They may unconsciously internalize those expectations and then play them out in their adult lives.

The shame of sexual molestation is a guilty stain that many in the pew carry. Many pew members dress up to church Sunday after Sunday to clothe the shame that lies beneath. But many victims know that once they get behind closed doors, the scar of childhood molestation robs their self worth. If only they can tell someone how they feel and what was done to them, and in response be told that "it was not your fault" – that shame would lose its hold as it is doing now.

There is something to be said about the power of voice. Talking about your guilt or shame can help you to move through the isolation that guilty stains create. The Bible tells us that life and death are in the power of the tongue (Proverbs 18:21, KJV). This verse speaks to a principle we have not fully grasped. The power of giving voice to the agony of guilt is a step toward victory. It is no wonder that some of the most gifted speakers of our time have had very difficult pasts. They have learned the power of voice and have no problem telling the world about the experiences they have endured and overcome. They have chosen not to be silent about past abuse and problems, and they have stepped over their negative obstacles. By doing so, they have helped others to break their silence and overcome their guilty stains through the power of Jesus Christ. One of the goals of the enemy is to keep you silent. You may not become a gifted speaker who can tell the world what you have gone through, but you can start by telling yourself what happened in your life that created the guilt you struggle with.

This may sound weird, but what if you wrote a letter to yourself describing the things you think you already know about yourself? Please try it, and include the things circling in your mind that you would never tell anyone. Yes, no one knows better than you what you are battling with in secret. Putting those hidden secrets on paper helps you pull those memories out of your mind, extract them, so you can better acknowledge them for what they are. And as an act of faith, this exercise can help you to expunge that guilt you are carrying and get it out in the open. If you give voice to that issue, you will begin to purge the guilty stains that come with it. As you write this letter that speaks to the hidden areas of your life, do it with prayer and faith. You may write things that shock you, but God is able to bring clarity and healing.

Writing is a form of healing. This art form is getting lost in our fast-paced, high-tech world. We write in shorthand in our e-mails and text messages, and we have moved away from pulling at the strings of our hearts with pen and paper. In Habakkuk 2:2 (KJV), we read:

And the LORD answered me, and said,
Write the vision, and make it plain upon tables,
that he may run that readeth it.

Habakkuk was told to write down the revelation so that others could read it and run with it. The revelation of God is in you. You may feel you are not equipped to work through the guilty stains you carry, but out of your spirit you can write the things that are hidden that only the Holy Spirit can reveal. Writing is an act of faith, and by doing it you can experience the revelatory word of God.

Once you write yourself a letter, put it in a confidential file in a private area of your home and read it back to yourself in two days. Then respond to that letter by writing another one to yourself that speaks about what you should do according to the word of God. Whatever you write, confirm that the Bible aligns with it—this is a must. This means that if you write that you want to end your life, you know this is outside the biblical mandate and it cannot be from God. Also, extract and memorize scripture verses from the bible that speaks of the promises of God. For example, Deuteronomy 28 and Isaiah 43 are very helpful passages that speaks of God's promises. You can Google the Bible on the internet and put in key words so you can find scriptures that deal with God's promises, his majesty & his power. Psalms & Proverbs are especially good chapter books to delve into as well. Why am I telling you to do this? Because you will be giving voice to those stains that are lingering in your mind, and by putting them on paper you are telling them it's laundry time! You're getting the bleach, which is the word of God, to wipe those guilty stains clean. In Isaiah 1:18 (KJV) it says:

Come now and let us reason together, saith the Lord:
though your sins be as scarlet they shall be as white as snow
though they be red like crimson they shall be as wool.

It may not be your sins that you need the Lord to make clean, but rather those secret traumas, regrets and lack of closure that have become imprisoned in your mind and need to be broken free. Tell the Lord about the situation that has held you bound. Talking and writing about your guilt is a way to release it. This may lead you to do things you previously did not have strength to do. You may have to tell someone you are sorry.

You may have to forgive. Perhaps, even, you may turn your life around and pursue the things you never thought possible.

God can give you the closure you need when you cannot get it from a particular person. He may push your mind towards other positive areas to pursue. Have you ever thought about going back to school? Pursuing a change of career? Planning for the purchase of your first home? Going on a missions trip? How exciting that would be? If necessary, God will send those friends we talked about in Chapter 3 into your radar. They may never know the depth of your circumstances, but through the inspiration of the Holy Spirit they can be instruments that let you know that God is going to take you through your trouble. Put your trust in Him. He will send the necessary reinforcements when you need them. Nobody can do what Christ can do, but if he chooses, he will put some special people into your life as instruments to bring forth healing to the glory of God.

Some of you have battled the guilt of having a child with some form of illness or disability, whether physical, mental or psychological. You may feel that some wrongdoing of yours caused this to happen. You may have experienced the stares from your church colleagues, the insensitive questions and the comments, all of which make it appear that you are being punished. You need to know that God knows you by name. The child who has been brought into the world through you was no mistake—this child has brought beauty into your life and taught you a depth of love no one else can understand.

You probably have a heightened sensitivity to others' needs because your child has brought out this very special quality in you. Parents who have nurtured children with disabilities learn skills that allow them to reach people in ways the average person cannot. You are blessed. You have done no wrong, there is nothing different you could have done, and you must accept what God has put in your life, for He knows what is in your future. Don't allow ignorant folk to bring on embarrassment, regret or shame. You are God's child and He will supply your every need—including patience, strength and ability. God is with you. Bless you and bless your child.

You may be suffering from the pain of losing a loved one. Every year on the anniversary of his/her death you plunge into depression as you rehearse their premature departure. You may say to yourself, "I should have done more, I should have been there, and I should have told them more often that I loved them. Those notions are guilty stains that have grown deep, and they are relived and rehashed for you to punish yourself. Celebrate your loved one's memory, but do not celebrate your pain. When you focus more on yourself than on his/her legacy, it becomes very hard to dissociate yourself from the pain of your loss. Working through grief is heart-wrenching. It takes time, reflection and healing. God will help you to get up from your brokenness and to understand your own commitment toward your daily walk with the Lord. Your loved one's death was never intended to slow you down. You may need to pause and reflect on their life and what they really meant to you, but God will take every step with you as you transition through this loss. As the song says:

> Each step I take I know that He will guide me—
> To higher ground He ever leads me on;
> Until some day the last step will be taken,
> Each step I take just leads me closer home.

Your grief can lead you to the higher ground of knowing where you are going. It is the memory of the loved one that can help you to pursue a promising life. But when you mix guilt with unending regret, it keeps the pain fresh, and it limits your potential to get to that higher ground in God. As you celebrate the loved one's legacy, the pain will be felt, but it will begin to subside. Preserve the positive memories, not the negative ones that keep your guilt in tact. One day, on that anniversary, the guilty stain will be no more.

Guilt can come from so many things. You may remember the warnings you were given to avoid certain situations, but to which you didn't listen at the time. You are listening now. You are listening to all the alarm bells of guilt clanging for more attention. The solution is to tell it to Jesus. If you choose the path of Calvary and believe in the atoning blood of Christ, I speak healing over that guilt that plagues you. In Genesis 1:3-4 (KJV) it reads:

> And God said, Let there be light: and there was light.
> And God saw the light, that it was good: and God divided
> the light from the darkness.

The Lord separated the light from the darkness. This tells us that we are children of the light and that we were not created to walk in darkness or to live in the dark areas of our lives where the light of God has not shone. I pray that God's illuminating light and power will pour into those darkened cells of your life that have held you in bondage. May the Lord loose a bright future in you and spiritual prosperity, and may your guilt be replaced with the freedom in God that equips you for your destiny. Calvary covered every sin, abuse and trauma. Break the silence and watch God work in your life.

We have all seen the way we have elevated people in our churches. Remember humble Helen? She was a character we discussed in Chapter 2. She was the person we have all seen in the church who does what she is told, yet lives in an abyss of regret. She is single, growing older and feels life has passed her by. Humble Helen is battling guilt that has not been given a voice. Like Humble Helen, we tend to put some people on a pedestal and advance them to the category of sainthood. What we do not realize is that this presents a serious quandary for those people and puts overwhelming pressure on them to be something they are not. It is difficult for them to deal with secret battles because, like humble Helen, they are expected to live perfect lives.

So many times in the church we see people who look the part, act the part and talk the part, but who live the exact opposite. The very thing they speak out against is the very thing they fall into. Their false life of perfection becomes a real life of imperfection. It is good to praise and recognize people, but we have to do that in a healthy way. We have to be careful about the way we elevate some over others. We also have to be mindful of the false expectations we put on people, because nothing is ever what it seems. In humble Helen's case, she hated the way the church pressured her, and she eventually grew bitter. She played into what they wanted her to be, but it stole her power of choice. She missed out on having a life with a husband and maybe children because of the church's false expectations and because she did not have the strength to stand up for herself in the church community.

There are many humble Helens in the church today. They come to church but they never truly experience it. Out of their obedience to the moral codes of the church, they do what they are told and never pursue their God-given desires because of people's expectations.

I have a vivid memory of an anointed and broadly respected woman in the church I once attended. I was about ten years old, and one Sunday morning this woman had an emotional breakdown right before the eyes of the congregation. She went to the altar and broke down in tears, sobbing about how bad her life had become. I remember wondering what it was that had made this strong anointed woman cry like a baby at the front of the church. A flock of people surrounded her as they fervently prayed for her, consoling her and telling her that everything was going to be all right. I couldn't understand why so many people were consoling this great woman of God. I'd never seen anything like that before. I had certainly seen people at the altar cry, but this scene was radically different. I knew something was seriously wrong and I remembered feeling very sad for her.

This woman was someone who would sing in the church with a melodious sound. She would exhort the word of God in excellence. She was highly respected, but it appeared that nobody knew the burden of guilt and unhappiness buried beneath her giving nature.

After that day, it became known in the church that the root cause of her breakdown was the guilt she carried for not living the life she really wanted. What she wanted was to be married. She wanted children like everyone else. She was a beautiful and intelligent woman. Waiting for the "right" man to come along, she had turned down numerous marriage proposals. As she aged, she grew lonely and began to think about the prospective husbands she had rejected. She may have reflected on what it would have been like to be the "first lady" of the church, for many of those previous suitors were said to be men who went on to be pastors and bishops. She may have wondered what it would have been like to be a mother herself when she gave encouragement to many mothers. She regretted her decisions immensely and couldn't see her life going on. She did recuperate, or so they say, but she was never the same from that day forward.

That image of her breaking down at the front of the church has been deeply imprinted in my mind for over 25 years. I now understand that the guilt she carried hit her that day like a ton of bricks. Her mind and body could no longer cope with those guilty stains. She could no longer repress them or pretend they weren't there. This led her inner alarm bell of guilt to ring out stridently, which manifested itself as a mental breakdown for all to see. Her body was telling her, "No more! I need to shut you down until you deal with these guilty stains!" We can only ask, how many more humble Helens are out there? How many more are sitting in our pews with guilt mounting like lava in a volcano, just waiting for enough pressure to erupt? Could one of them be you?

We must give people room to be real, to be who they are. Otherwise, some are forced to lead a double life, one real, one not, until the guilt they live with erupts. People must be nurtured in environments where they can experience their heart's desire in God. In Psalms 37:4 (KJV) it says:

> Delight thyself also in the LORD:
> and he shall give thee the desires of thine heart.

It is important that we strive to be happy in church and seek out the things that bring delight in God. The degree of shock we experience when a highly regarded church member falls creates canyons of guilt for the church community to deal with. My story of the woman who broke down at the altar reminds us of how easy it is to overlook such pew members and also that we should encourage everyone—regardless of the roles they play in our pulpits and our pews. When we make statements like, they're holier than thou or too holy and stuff like that, we give no space for these vessels, like humble Helen, to be restored. Remember, in many instances they fall because the expectations we put on them block out who they really are.

Another area to consider is this: the people we hold in high esteem in the church can become arrogant about their secret failings because they are angry within their spirit about the way they have been treated. Not in the sense of being slandered, but rather because of the image that has been created for them to live up to. Too often we see people fall, for example, into sexual sin (particularly leaders in the church), without formally acknowledging their errors and attempting to return as quickly as possible to the right path instead. As we look on them, we wonder why they are not able to humble themselves, acknowledge their sin and remove themselves from that leadership post even for a while. I sometimes think it's because they do not know what other way to behave as they struggle to live up to the expectations others have put on them. Perhaps they have never seen anyone in the church plunge from status to failure and get back up again. They do not know how to deal with their *real* selves when the expectations have been to do otherwise. They are like fish outside the fish bowl, gasping to return to their environment of expectation. They may feel they can't come down off their pedestal because they do not know what they will encounter when they do. Instead, they may fall to sin, never deal with it and remain in leadership roles with guilty stains that one day will violently demand a response.

The private pains people carry are kept private because the environment is not conducive to being open or real. If we never hear the reality of someone else's life, if we never know that someone else experienced abuse and overcame it, or if we never witness someone else make it through grief, embarrassment or bewilderment, it is no surprise that we remain the way we are. Have people in the pews overcome these tragedies – of course! But unfortunately we never hear those stories.

We must seek to be humble in this life and to recognize that we are who we are because of God's grace. We need to consider others and not elevate people excessively, because we all have dreams, aspirations and desires, and we all can make mistakes. Our guilty stains are not always about the individual, but they can be inflicted by others and what people think about fallen vessels within the church. Every time we mention another holy roller, let's remember the humble Helens in our circle who want to be real just like everybody else.

There are two specific types of guilt that are important to tackle. The first is the guilt that comes as a result of sin against God, and the second is the guilt fueled by the enemy. The following sections will take us through these two types and provide some insight into how we can overcome the guilty stains.

Guilt caused by sin

In Mark 3:28 (KJV), Jesus declares:

> Verily I say unto you, all sins shall be forgiven unto the sons of men, and blasphemies wherewith soever they shall blaspheme.

This verse tells us that the only sin that is not forgivable is blasphemy against the Holy Ghost. Once a person repents, he or she is pardoned for every wrongdoing. My famous statement goes like this: if you killed ten men, chopped them up in pieces, and buried them somewhere, then acknowledged and were sorrowful for your heinous act and were willing to face the judgment, God said that He can forgive even that horrible crime. As unfathomable as this crime may be, Jesus can forgive any sinner. The despicable act I've used in this example is not intended to diminish the atrocity of such a crime or to trivialize the suffering of victims of violence, but to understand the extent to which God can forgive a person.

If an individual is truly sorrowful for his sin and turns to God for forgiveness, he will be heard. As Christians, however, we have made some sins out to be so hellish and unforgivable that we give mixed messages to the person who has fallen. We have come down so hard on certain sins that even if you have been forgiven by God, you feel you have not been forgiven by people. It could be something that happened so long ago you should be able to just forget it, but you can't. You may torture yourself by wondering how you could have allowed certain things to turn out the way they did. You may ask yourself so many questions that the guilt you feel as a result has emotionally drained you.

Opening doors to sin is not as easy as closing doors to sin. You may clap, sing and shout, but you know you can only go so far. You attend church and have a great time, too, but as soon as you get behind closed doors, you crumble like sand that was thought to be a stone. Continuing to participate in the hypocrisy of living a life of sin without repentance is draining both physically and spiritually. The guilt reminds you that there is something you need to correct. Why not listen to that small voice? Why not end that affair, call that friend, confess that sin to God so He can help you and forgive you?

Tracing your guilt to its cause can help you to connect, as well, with other areas that you may be struggling with. For example, the habit of sowing discord and creating contention is sometimes an indication of an underlying sorrow or an abusive past. The person who is always in disputes, quarrels and misunderstandings is something the Lord abhors. The word of God says that he who sows discord is an abomination to the Lord (Proverbs 6:16). However, if you trace the sin of inciting discord to the guilt that a person carries in other areas of life, you may be able to find the root of this destructive behaviour. What is he or she so mad about? Is a question you should ask. If you dig beneath this angry behaviour, you may find that this person has had negative encounters with an authority figure. It could have been a teacher, relative, parent or a caregiver who did not nurture the person in a positive way, perhaps focusing on only negative traits, such as a bad attitude, lack of smarts, or unattractive physical features—and this in turn has created hurt within that person. She may feel unworthy and frustrated, and may wonder why she reacts so strongly to any form of criticism.

A person subjected to negativity from an authority figure for a large part of his life may have a battered self-worth that sours his ability to get along with people. He may carry deep resentment and anger toward anyone who reminds him of this authority figure or who disapproves of who he wants to be. As a coping mechanism, this person feels he has to appear strong, and thus stirs up contentions and wars to prevent this circumstance from happening again. He prefers not to be the recipient of slander, so he becomes the one doing the accusing and slandering. And so, getting to the root of the bad behaviour can unlock his deep passion, which is, coincidentally, a deep passion for people. It is this deep-rooted anger and resentment that is getting in the way of fostering balanced relationships with others, and it needs to be dealt with in order to understand the positive attributes that God has given this person as His child. Their angry behaviour can be related to a number of hidden things in their past, like physical, sexual or emotional abuse to name a few. Whatever the problem, if we can tease out the guilt of a person's past and connect it to the problem of their present, we can effectively help them to turn things around.

When you sin, you should feel guilt and shame. If you find yourself in a perpetually sinful situation and you no longer feel guilty about your actions, you are probably on the way to being publicly exposed. You can only do something for so long and get away with it. When bad behaviours continue and become chronic, only a drastic measure, like a lightning bolt (metaphorically speaking), will get your attention. God prefers that we exercise our free will to abandon sin and turn to Him.

To be reconciled with God, you must acknowledge that something is wrong and work to make it right. If you continue on a path of sin, you will inevitably meet up with disaster, and you should never wait for that to happen. Disaster can get you back on course all right, but it's a hard lesson to learn and not everyone makes it out alive spiritually. You can keep your spirit alive by constantly refreshing your moral compass, which can be done through prayer, church participation and honesty with yourself. Guilt keeps us honest about what we've done and what needs to be done to get right with God. You will never move to the next dimension till you address the sin in your life. Confess to God. A broken and contrite heart He will not despise. The price that Jesus paid at Calvary was paid to pull your life out of the ridicule and accusation of the devil. Listen to those alarm bells of guilt that keep you able to hear the voice of God. Guilt from sin is not a place in which you need to remain. God has made a way of escape for you. Follow His plan for your life.

Guilt caused by the adversary

Guilt is a natural human condition, and it helps to guide us to what is important in our lives. However, not everything that makes us feel guilty is the result of our wrongdoings. The Devil repeatedly tells lies to the saints, saying that their guilty stains cannot be removed—and this cripples people from moving from point A to point B. Every time you try to push forward, that guilt creeps up on you like a predator stalking its prey. The enemy accuses you of your past and declares your weaknesses eternal impediments that will block you from working for God. He repeats this until you accept his accusations and declarations as truths. But the accusations the devil makes have nothing to do with you! They are an attack on the kingdom of God, a means to turn the hearts and minds of His people away from the gift of salvation, which justifies and sanctifies them as believers.

The person, who has repented of their sin but continues to feel guilty day after day, even after their sins have been forgiven, is facing a stronghold. A stronghold is a lie that is believed. If we allow ourselves to fall into this trap the enemy sets, we create doors through which he can enter. The stronghold of guilt is usually accompanied with an incorrect perception of ourselves or an incorrect perception of God (which are both strongholds in themselves). When these feelings come upon you, it is important to ask: is the guilt I am feeling about the sin in my life I have already repented for? If it is, the devil may be trying to implant a spirit of guilt and accusation.

It is important that you understand the victory of the cross as distinct from the death of the cross. The death of the cross symbolizes the condemnation to sin while the victory of the cross (the resurrection of Jesus Christ) symbolizes the overcoming of sin. People who have a stronghold of guilt rarely see God for His awesome forgiving nature, or they don't see themselves correctly. Satan's job is to torment God's people by reminding them of their past failures so he can bring on guilt that creates strongholds of depression. We have to be extremely careful about whom we allow to breathe into our spirit, and we must also be aware of false prophets who may come to us saying they have the word of the Lord.

In order to plant strongholds in us, the enemy can work through people to accuse us of things in our past that have already been dealt with and buried under the blood of Jesus. This is a spirit of false accusation that has infiltrated the church. It is a demonic spirit that must be rebuked, as it tries to dig up what is already dead. This spirit seeks to mimic the resurrection power of Jesus Christ. Only God has the power to raise the dead to life. Spiritually speaking, if God has forgiven you and helped you work through issues in your past and accordingly has pronounced them dead, then nothing, no person and no demon, has the authority to bring these dead issues back to life. So any time a previously dealt-with event tries to reawaken itself, you can take this as a sign that a satanic attack is mimicking the resurrection power. Assume authority and let that devil know that Jesus Christ already took the keys of death, hell and the grave. Remember, the goal of this demonic spirit is to make you think you are still bound by past mistakes and to keep you in a state of guilt.

I can recall being approached by an individual who tried to remind me of a guilty stain in my past that God had already dealt with. This person told me to do something that was contrary to every word the Lord has ever spoken to me. I stood my ground and kept to the word of the Lord. I instantly recalled the scripts of my life, the visitations from God, the supernatural experiences and the Scriptures that the Lord had given me over the years. As I listened to these words of prophecy, my life script flashed before my eyes. I attempted to apply the word (Isaiah 28:10) this individual was giving me to see if I could match it line by line and precept by precept to what God had previously told me. But what the individual said to me did not fall in line by line or precept by precept. In fact, it would erase every Scripture, visitation and word I had ever received from the Lord. What this person said to me as a "word of prophecy" did not match up with God's word. 1 John 1:4 (KJV) warns us:

> Beloved, believe not every spirit,
> but try the spirits whether they are of God:
> because many false prophets are gone out into the world.

There is a principle we must always follow. God does not speak outside of His word and He is not the author of confusion. You must know the voice of God as distinct from the voice of the devil. This comes with knowledge of the word of God and a consecrated life that is committed to hearing from the Lord. Do not receive and accept every word that is spoken in your life, for there are many false prophets, as John reminds us, that have gone into the world. You must prove and test the word of God. This is why it is important to have an established prayer life where God can speak to you and warn you of impending danger. If you accept false prophecy, it can mess up your spirit and create guilty stains that keep you locked down. Consider what the prophet Ezekiel says in 13:22 (KJV):

> Because with lies ye have made the heart of the righteous
> sad, whom I have not made sad; and strengthened the
> hands of the wicked, that he should not return from his
> wicked way, by promising him life;

This speaks to the false prophets who tell things to people that bring sadness upon them, but this sadness is not from God. It speaks to how the hands of the wicked are being strengthened, when this is not what God approves.

Weeks before my experience with that individual, the Lord had given me several scriptures that dealt with prophecy and false prophets. I had journaled the scriptures with a question: Why, Lord, do you keep giving me scriptures about prophecy and false prophets? I prayed about this and asked the Lord what He wanted me to know. I did not get an answer and did not understand what He was showing me until I was approached at that moment by the false prophet. The enemy will try to bring accusations into your life, and you have to know who you belong to and what authority you acknowledge. You must know without a shadow of a doubt that God is your authority and you must stand on what He has spoken to you. No demon can circumvent your experiences with God. A demon will try to accuse you, but you must stand on the word of God, which brought you life, forgiveness and removal of every guilty stain. The enemy will twist words and make them appear as if they are God's, just as he did when he tempted Eve in the Garden of Eden.

Boldly, I let the person know that what they received was not from God. It did concern me that this person had allowed their spirit to be channeled by a spirit of false prophecy. I decided not to breathe oxygen into what they told me to do, for their words were designed to infect my spirit. We parted on that note, and in no less than 24 hours, a very old man in the church approached me. He and I had never exchanged words other than a "Praise the Lord." A tear formed in his eye as he touched my hand and told me I was blessed. He proceeded to repeat that I was blessed for what seemed like 30 times. I had been told this before, but that day I heard something different in the spirit as this old man kept repeating, "You are blessed." He began to pray for me under the inspiration of the Lord. He reaffirmed the word of God in my life and told me to press on and to do what I am doing for God. That tear I'd noticed eventually ran down the right side of his face as he blessed me and pronounced the benediction of the Lord on my life, which says:

> The LORD bless thee, and keep thee:
> The LORD make his face shine upon thee, and be
> gracious unto thee:
> The LORD lift up his countenance upon thee, and give
> thee peace. …In Jesus' name. (Numbers 6:24 KJV)

I went home, prayed and thanked God for the true prophetic words in my life. I do not know why God used a man more than twice my age and physically shaky and weak. But this man's counsel and prayer were full of strength, truth and virtue. I believe this old man was strategically placed in my life for that exact moment. He had listened to the voice of God and counteracted the enemy's assault on me.

It makes me think of the aged saints in the church who believe they are dried up with no purpose. You may be elderly and feel your days are numbered, but I want you to know that even the very old and infirm can hear the voice of God. You have the experience, knowledge and endurance. You may also still live with certain guilty stains from your past, because you may feel you are forgotten and have little use in the kingdom of God. Your experience and wisdom are needed. I want you to know that, like that elderly man, you can keep your spirit strong. Know that your present days can have an impact on someone's life, such as what happened with me. When we are being attacked by the devil, we will need seasoned people in the church to help pray us through. If you still carry those regrets, you cannot effectively pass on the wisdom and blessing that someone much younger than you will need. That old man's body may have been weak, but that day he was mightily used of the Lord, and it will go down in my archives of His visitation.

During a prayer of thanks to the Lord, a fresh prophetic word came into my spirit. In the space of 24 hours I had received a false prophecy, which was quickly counteracted by the word of God, who spoke new things into my life. I received a release to pursue another area of ministry I had never contemplated. I firmly believe that if God had not given me that warning in those scriptures prior to that incident, and if He had not given me that blessing after it, that demonic word might have infiltrated my spirit in a way that could have annihilated my destiny. Be certain that you are grounded in God and know that the enemy is looking to accuse you of the things that are a lie. Guilty stains can be invoked by the enemy. It is important that you know the difference between the guilt of sin and the guilt that comes from satanic forces, for the latter must be cast out in the name of Jesus. You are set free by the liberating word of God.

Lose all your guilty stains

Never underestimate the realities of unresolved hurt and pain. If you find that you are having severe difficulty overcoming past experiences, that the guilt from past traumas is crippling you, it's often an indication that you have not properly dealt with the event or events that caused the guilt. You have not been set free. If you also feel that you are struggling with immense shame, you probably need to get some help from a professional Christian counsellor. There are some situations that people pass through that demand professional skill. Be diligent in pursuing and seeking such resources. Check with your local church to see if there are Christian counsellors you could meet with, or check Christian directories or websites for the resources you require. Don't battle things on your own. We are body, soul and spirit. We may be able to get the spiritual deliverance that reconciles us with God, but matching our psychological and mental health to our spiritual health and being made whole may require intervention.

Signs of unresolved pain and trauma include the following:

- loss of appetite for no reason at all
- difficulty maintaining healthy relationships
- lack of sexual interest or obsessive sexual interest
- being extremely emotional without understanding why, e.g., outbursts of crying
- depression and anxiety
- difficulty with forgiveness
- loss of memory, blackouts or only a vague memory of childhood.

Our guilt can be dealt with through the word of God. If it is guilt for wrongdoing, the word of God rightly declares that a "broken and a contrite heart He will not despise" (Psalms 51:17, KJV).

If it is guilt from the adversary, you can apply the word of God that says:

> Therefore if any man be in Christ.
> he is a new creature; old things are passed away;
> Behold, all things are become new (2 Corinthians 5:17, KJV).

Guilt is one of the enemy's greatest weapons. The devil wants to tear you down and tell you lies so that your faith and confidence in God are compromised. But God is your defence. He is able to counteract every weapon the enemy tries to use against you.

Guilt should never reach the point of crippling the Christian if he or she seeks help. Get the proper counsel to help you work to connect the dots in your life so you can understand who you are and match that with *whose* you are. Then you can relinquish the pain that preceded the very act about which you feel guilty.

Jesus never intended your mistakes to paralyze you to the point of living an unhappy Christian life. Take that step and lose all your guilty stains when you identify with Christ our Lord. Don't pull away from God, regardless of what you are going through. The Bible tells us to

> …draw near with a true heart in full assurance of faith, having our hearts sprinkled from an evil conscience… (Hebrews 10:22, KJV)

Believe that God is able to keep you from falling. Believe that He can make you whole in every aspect of your life. You may be struggling with one or more of the following:

- a broken relationship
- viewing pornography
- the death of a loved one
- marriage to a person you do not love
- unwanted singleness
- an abortion
- being a victim of molestation
- having a disabled child
- being a victim of physical and verbal abuse
- unwanted fantasies of same-sex relationships
- committing adultery
- a bad profession
- having an affair with a married person
- telling a lie that cost a friendship
- making a wrong decision
- the inability to bear children
- having a child out of wedlock.

Jesus can deal with every one of these and more. Don't continue to replay the events that have caused guilt to cripple you. Instead, tell the movie you have created that there is a new producer, a new screenwriter and a new executive in charge. That new person is Jesus. He will write your script and he will produce your movie and the outcome will be a guilt-free life that embraces all the possibilities in Christ. Jesus Christ died so that you can lose all your guilty stains. He died so you could be released from everything that has held you in bondage. Be free and delivered from your past. Come out of the stain of guilt. Jesus already paid that price. Believe it and embrace your renewed life!

*For I am poor and needy, and my heart is
wounded within me.
(Psalm 109:22 NIV)*

Chapter 5

Wounds that Won't Heal

Now that you understand what guilty stains mean and how you can best address them, it seems that for every step forward you take, you take two steps backward! It's as if there is a world going on that you are watching but are not a part of. The situations you have passed through have been tough, hard, painful and so wrong—and you think that if you ever let out the ocean of tears behind the levees of your heart, you're not sure you'll be able to stop the flow. And so you conclude that it is better to just drop a tear here and there because those wounds you carry run too deep. This chapter may not speak to everyone. It is specifically written for those individuals who feel that they have been forgotten. It is written for those who are yearning for closure with people who have wounded them deeply and for those who have been waiting to hear those precious three words "I am sorry."

Indeed, your life has been hard and it is not what you'd thought it would be, so you carry on just because. In the church we are not allowed to stay in that place of pain for too long, for someone will tell you that "Yes, life is hard but God is good." Let's be real church folk. We all know that God is good. He is good all the time and that will never change! But to someone who is struggling and needs some acknowledgment of their pain, being told that "God is good" is something they already know. We make such statements simply so that we can move quickly through the awkward moments of emotion and not feel obliged to then ask the question "Why is life so hard for you?" Because the truth is we don't really want to know, and if we did, like that Sunday-school teacher who broke under the pressure with Samantha in chapter 2, many would not be able to handle the details. If you recall, the Sunday School teacher really did not want to help Samantha. If he did, he would have referred her to someone that was skilled to help her and Samantha's wounds would not have become worse.

When Hurricane Katrina caused the levees of New Orleans to break on August 29, 2005, more than 1800 people lost their lives. Prior to Katrina, many wondered if these levees could withstand the perfect storm. After all, they were built over fifty years ago and were in desperate need of repair. They had held up for many years against the constant battering of the Mississippi River, and while they'd never been brought to the standards of the twenty-first century, many thought they would continue to hold up. But in August 2005, Katrina proved them wrong. The levees protecting the residents of New Orleans had had enough. The warnings, speculations and predictions of its unsafe infrastructure had been ignored by those in charge, and their silence resulted in a catastrophic failure. That choice to be silent screams loudly today. Once the winds started to roar in August 2005 and the waves hit them like never before, the levees were history.

Some speculate that because many of the residents of New Orleans were poor and black, they were not worth the attention and the expense to ensure a safe environment. It wasn't until Hurricane Katrina hit New Orleans that the world got a glimpse of the way people had lived prior to the storm. The degree of poverty in the city made the place seem like the Third World. The residents of New Orleans were rich in spirit to survive in such socio-economic hardships—but when Katrina hit, their impoverishment and lack of support were out there for all to see and resulted in many losing their lives.

I use the Katrina disaster as an analogy of the conditions in the church today. We are rich in spirit, but we have become impoverished as a Christian community because we fail to cater to the immediate needs of our pew members. Just as the Mississippi River pushed against the levees, the enemy, is violently pushing against the walls of the church. The levees of the church have grown weak, and if the perfect storm should arise, casualties are almost certain.

To understand the spiritual application of the Mississippi River we must understand the river's natural significance. One of the most powerful rivers in the world, the Mississippi is the longest river in the United States and probably the most revered and referred-to river in North America. It plays an important part in slave narratives, songs and historical documents. Over the centuries, the flow of the Mississippi River has been compromised by manmade levees (a levee is a type of damn or embankment that prevents a river from overflowing) that either stops the flow of the river in certain areas or redirects it to allow for people to live habitably in certain regions. The Mississippi *has* overflown its banks before in history; however, Katrina was a reminder of how ferocious the current of that river really is.

The forceful flow of the Mississippi River is useful for understanding the emotional state of those with deep wounds. There are rivers of hurt that flow within some of you, and the Holy Spirit is the levee that has prevented the overflow of this hurt, which might lead to a breakdown. Like the levee, the Holy Spirit stops the onslaught of the enemy that wants to overtake your ship. It redirects and stops the current of your past so that you can live habitably in victory as God's special child. You must, however, ensure that the levees of your spirit hold strong. They will if you let the word of God refresh you. The Holy Spirit must work through the life of every believer so that levees are fortified and brought up to the standard that will withhold against storms. Your levees are types of walls that give you spiritual protection—not to be confused with walls we create to keep people away—to fight and address those deep wounds that hinder your progress. You may feel that your levees are giving way to the storms mounting within you, so you must feed and encourage the Holy Spirit to work in your life with force and conviction to stop the flow.

To know that someone in our pews has been lied to with no recourse, or that some child has been fondled by an adult parishioner, or that someone has stolen money that belongs to the Lord and do nothing is a breach of our levees. If we had addressed the men who carried on multiple simultaneous relationships with women in the church, if we had ex-communicated and reported the pedophiles that lurked behind white clergy collars, we would not have had so many wounded soldiers in our pews. Every time we fail to address issues in our church, our levees become weaker. Our levees need repair. If government officials at the time of Katrina had tuned into the conditions of New Orleans and repaired the levees, lives would have been saved. If our churches had responded to the silent screams of pew members and had punished the acts of indiscretion, so many soldiers in Christ would not have died.

In Nehemiah Chapter 3, we have the biblical account of the prophet's desire to rebuild the walls of Jerusalem. As an assistant to a king, Nehemiah used his influence to get permission to return to his homeland and rebuild the walls that had been burned down. Walls in the ancient cities were forms of protection and defence against intruders who would try to overtake a city and enslave the people of God. Nehemiah refused to accept this fate for his people and he refused to let the legacy of his forefathers lie in waste. He knew that if the walls remained broken down, his people would be left vulnerable to the surrounding enemies. Therefore, he gathered his people to rebuild the walls. Nehemiah had to withstand the criticisms of those who opposed the success of God's people—but he built the walls nevertheless, nail and hammer in one hand and faith in God in the other. This biblical passage is relevant to us today. We must realize that our church walls are burned down just as Nehemiah did, and come together to rebuild the walls.

We cannot effectively fight as soldiers when we have wounds that won't heal. The wounds that many carry in the church are like the putrefying sores about which Isaiah 1:6 (KJV) tells us:

> From the sole of the foot even unto the head there is no soundness in it; but wounds, and bruises, and putrefying sores: they have not been closed, neither bound up, neither mollified with ointment.

The prophet Isaiah describes a disturbing condition within the church. He speaks to a people who have gone backward and recognizes the need to address the unhealthy state within the body of Christ. A sore, as Isaiah says, is the residue of the flesh that has been punctured. A sore could be the result of an infection, and this discomfort and pain gives a constant reminder that something needs to be attended to. The passage in Isaiah helps us to understand that the church is being called out to address the wounds within the body. This passage also triggers in us the question: how do we heal putrefying sores that are resistant to treatment? The answer, in part, lies in the cracking levees of our churches, families and personal lives.

As a church community we need to do more to rebuild the levees of the church, because the storm is forming, the waves are dashing high and the church is not equipped. Have you ever wondered why people in our churches are suffering from ailments, depression and anxiety at alarming rates? Or why so many churches have experienced splits in the past twenty years? Putrefying sores within the body of Christ that have been left unattended. As a result, we have wounds that won't heal, and that cause the amputations of church structures, fellowship, relationships and health.

Like Linda, the church administrative assistant in chapter 2 who became severely depressed because of the way she was handled, there are pew members in similar situations who have been ill treated. They come to church, but they can no longer weather the storms because of the breaches in the levees of the church. Linda internalized the hurt she experienced in the church, and this mutated to a condition that could lead to cancer. The internalization of pain, which causes stress that can lead to certain diseases, is very real. How many funerals have we attended where the "cause of death" was accompanied by whisperings of the stress, malice and infidelities of the deceased? But, *shh*, we are never supposed to engage in real talk about the private miseries or indiscretions of those who have passed on.

The wounds that won't heal include emotional scars of unforgiveness that are induced when we don't care about what has happened to our fellow church brethren. We have overlooked the "strong" ones like Linda, humble Helen and the Sunday-school teacher, all of whom internalized their struggles. Like the levees breached by Katrina, it was not until the perfect storm came that they crumbled under the devastation of a fall, depression or illness.

As church members, we should not wait for a catastrophic event before we realize we must repair the levees. We should encourage skilled individuals to get accredited, educated and immersed in the ministry of counsel. We must hold people accountable for wrongful acts committed against members of the church. We must strategize and stand firm on dealing with people guilty of behaviour that has deeply affected others within the church. We must insist that those who refuse to abide by the biblical codes of conduct be accountable. We must act. Our soldiers are wounded and they do not have the strength to withstand the battering that will inevitably come.

I once heard about a woman in the church who had a problem with forgiveness. Thirty years ago she had loaned someone in a high-ranking position in the church a large sum of money that was never repaid. As the years passed she waited for the person to at the very least explain what had happened. The three words "I am sorry" would have been a nice start, especially as she watched them move from one house to a bigger, more costly one. The day never came when she heard those three words, and she grew bitter as she witnessed what appeared to be their success. Perhaps, having the funds returned meant less to her than being treated as if she mattered. She did not get the closure she sought and this frustrated her efforts to purchase her own home. She saw other church members purchase their homes as she waited for almost thirty years to get some acknowledgment of what was done to her. Although this woman was right to feel mistreated, the bitterness that grew within her caused her to lose out in life. The person who took her money and proved themselves lacking in integrity had moved on, while she was left in limbo by what that person had done.

The church has seen many such stories, one after the other, where money concerns have been mishandled. People have loaned money to friends and the church with little to no acknowledgment when things go wrong. The pocket-with-holes ministries—churches that are unable to maintain wealth, as money goes out just as quickly as it comes in—are the result of this type of ill conduct. The church does not lack the blessings our heavenly Father has brought us, but the tyranny of mismanagement and the misappropriation of money leaves a curse on church ministries that prevents them from accumulating the wealth that the prosperity gospel has promised them. This financial mismanagement is a condition that plagues so many churches today. People will continue to give and tithe from their earnings, for this is a biblical mandate; however, the pocket-with-holes ministries will never be chosen as God's stewards to handle wealth and push the Gospel, because they have not been honest and just in the way they have handled His people and their money.

The putrefying sores from which the woman who waited for thirty years suffered were bitterness, unforgiveness and anger. These wounds would not heal as she waited fruitlessly and she took her focus off of God, and thus He could not help her heal. It would entail an army battalion to rescue the wounded soldiers in the church. This is because there are so many fallen soldiers that there are fewer voluntary recruits equipped for God's army. The people who have unresolved issues will invariably wear a mask with pride; they may feel justified in wearing the mask because they say, "No one will ever hurt me that way again." They may still come to church and sit in the pews, but their destinies are locked with padlocks of distrust.

And to those of you who have refused to address your own inclinations or repay your debts or have used arrogant methods to step over someone and thus put a clog in the engine of the church, I ask, how could you take money from someone and not repay them? Or how could you sleep with that sister, push her aside and move on as if she was just a prostitute? Or why did you entice a man who is someone else's husband and claim them as your own? How could you do such a thing and not say you are sorry? Whatever the circumstance, some people need to hear those words, and when they don't, they become other wounded soldiers left unattended, for they have been wounded by people within the church who have refused to address their crap.

Untreated wounds release odours or stenches that attract demonic spirits sent to torment you. So if you have wounds that won't heal, you must extend forgiveness to every individual who has hurt you. Spiritually speaking, true forgiveness brings out a sweet-smelling odour that allows the angels of the Lord to come to your defence. But where bad odours of bitterness and unforgiveness dwell, the ministering angels of healing back away and don't treat the wounds. Do not wait for anyone to tell you they're sorry. If they do, great. If they don't, you can't wait! Demonstrate forgiveness and pay attention to any putrefying sores you've been suppressing or avoiding. These sores may be wounds of affliction, wounds of guilt, wounds of fear, wounds of self-loathing, wounds of sexual infidelity, wounds of sexual trauma, wounds of molestation, wounds of failed relationships or wounds of childhood abandonment. The list can go on and on, but it is up to you to not allow it to steal your future.

I want to introduce you to a woman with putrefying sores that would not heal. You will see how her unresolved hurts continued with her throughout her life and how, as she neared her late middle age, she made a decision that brought her to rock bottom.

Listen in.

Teresa Badger is a single mother of three daughters and two sons. After twelve years of marriage she found out that her husband had been unfaithful to her. She discovered this not from her husband confessing, but from the arrival of a child of her husband's she did not bear. When Teresa and her husband had immigrated to Canada, they had little more than the clothes on their backs. Teresa worked menial jobs and combined all her earnings with her husband's to build a good life, which later resulted in a big house and a car. They steadily moved up the social ranks in their community. They became a prominent family in the church and afforded a safe haven for many.

Teresa helped needful women in the church. She allowed them to stay in her home, provided food for them and also gave advice to them until they were financially stable enough to venture out on their own. One woman she brought into her home, however, had an affair with her husband. To make a long story short, the woman gave birth, and Teresa's husband went to live with this woman and his baby, and Teresa was left to raise the five children on her own. She was thirty-two and had no time to grieve her broken marriage, as she had young children to care for and she wanted to bring as much normalcy to their lives as she possibly could.

Teresa moved from her big house to social housing, because that was all she could afford. Although she often wondered how her husband could have betrayed her so cruelly, because her life had changed so abruptly and so fast she was forced to move on with no closure. Her only communication with her ex-husband was through a lawyer at the time of their separation and later divorce. Every time a bill came in or a child needed new shoes or new clothes, her anger became deeper and deeper.

As her children grew older, Teresa began to get very lonely. When she was thirty-five, her neighbour's brother, Stewart, took an interest in her and they developed a relationship. By this time, her older children were preparing for high school and her youngest child was now eleven. Stewart then began taking a perverse interest in her youngest. Teresa never tuned in. She was too happy just having a man in her life! But sadly, while she was at work, he started fondling her daughter. He threatened the child that if she ever told her mother, she would not believe her and would stop loving her because of the lie.

Teresa loved Stewart so much that she started to provide for him financially. She co-signed a car loan for him and they drove together in style. In the meantime, she noticed her youngest daughter was becoming extremely rebellious. Teresa began to get calls from the girl's school concerning her bad behaviour and provocative dress, and she tried and tried to get through to her daughter but to no avail. Teresa couldn't take it anymore. The constant fighting with her daughter was draining her and she needed to focus on her relationship with her boyfriend. In the heat of a fight with her daughter one day, tears welled up in her daughter's eyes and she screamed that Stewart had been touching her in her private areas. Teresa yelled back and called her a liar saying that she was rebellious and would get what she was looking for like burning in hell. Her daughter's tears dried up instantly and she said nothing more from that day forward.

Teresa continued in her relationship with Stewart and waited for him to pop the question. That question never came and he eventually moved away and married another woman in another city. By this time her youngest daughter had left home (she was fifteen). Teresa continued on, hurt and desperate for a companion. She was now thirty-nine. Teresa attended church, but her children were far more involved than she was. Her sons were musicians in the church and her two older daughters were similarly involved in church programs. The youngest was the only one not in the church.

Several years passed and Teresa was now forty-seven. A close friend outside the church had introduced her to an older unmarried fellow named Paul. He seemed to be the one. He was very attentive to Teresa and she grew fond of him. Not wanting to lose him, she cooked and cleaned for him and pushed her way into his life. To maintain his attention and care, she would often make up stories about how sick she was, This eventually wore on him—Teresa had become very needy and burdensome—and after two years he moved to a city across the country to get away from her. Teresa decided she had better follow him. She announced to her family that she wanted a change and would relocate them 3000 miles away. Her older sons were very entrenched in the church and felt it was a bad move. Teresa was adamant, however; she was moving and they were coming with her. She never told them it was because of Paul, but they suspected it was, although they didn't dare to say so.

In retaliation, her sons called a meeting with the elders of the church to see if they could talk some sense into Teresa. The elders knew of Teresa's past and her failed marriage. Her children continued to try to convince their mother not to move away. All their friends were in the church and they were happy where they were. Finally, a minister of the church who had known Teresa for many years came to talk to her. He spoke to her about the importance of stability for the children and how her relocating them so far away was not the best decision. It took the minister much convincing, but Teresa finally agreed to stay.

Almost thirteen years passed. Teresa was fifty-nine and her children were grown. She had never had another shot at being with someone. She was proud of the accomplishments of her sons and daughters, but over time she grew resentful of the lives they had that she was not able to have. She despised the relationship her children had with their father, who had remarried. They did not understand the depth of the pain their mother had suffered because of their father's departure. Nor did they seem to realize how hard it had been for Teresa to raise them on her own, with little financial support from their father. Her children were all married now except for her youngest daughter, and Teresa had grandchildren in the double digits. It seemed that everyone had moved on. Her ex was remarried, her children had their spouses and she was left alone. Even in her older age, she still wanted someone in her life.

Teresa had grown severely depressed. She'd soon be sixty, and her phone calls to her children were usually about ailments she thought she had and her lack of money. Like Paul, her children grew weary of hearing the same litany day after day. They eventually began not returning her calls. Teresa's loneliness grew like a cancer and she was scared of being alone.

Then Teresa met someone fifteen years older and she announced to her family that she would marry him. All her children fiercely opposed the idea and she backed off. Two years later Teresa started to correspond with a family friend named Arnold, who lived in another country. Over time, they grew fond of each other. She thought *he* could be the one, but unbeknownst to Teresa, Arnold had made a pass at her married daughter when she and her husband had visited him while on a trip to the country where the fellow lived. The daughter told Teresa about this incident when she realized that her mother was developing a relationship with the man, but Teresa refused to believe her, just as she had refused to believe her youngest daughter when she told her about Stewart's abuse. Teresa insisted that, with everyone else moving on with their lives, it was her time to be happy. So she decided to take the plunge. She managed to convince Arnold, who by the way was significantly younger than she was, that they should get married. She announced her intentions to her children and they expressed violent opposition to the plan. You ask why this time? Well, several reasons. First, the aforementioned inappropriate pass Arnold had made, he has a history of drug addiction, and the fact that he was fifteen years younger and had had no job for the past six years! Her children wanted her to be happy with someone, but this man did not fit the bill.

Teresa, meanwhile, believed that everyone needed a second chance in life and she was willing to give him that chance. And so her children did the same thing they did when Teresa had wanted to move across the country to be with Paul. They went to the elders of the church to talk sense into her, but this time Teresa would not listen. They had a family meeting to discuss her intentions, but Teresa was cold and unresponsive. Her sole purpose was to find someone who would support her marriage, but no one came forth. Two weeks later she left the country to marry the man. Her children heard about her plan the day she was to leave and they confronted her. But nothing could move Teresa, so determined was she to do what she wanted. Her children subsequently prayed for Teresa and asked God for a divine intervention.

Teresa boarded the plane to meet her future husband. Finally, she thought, despite being burdened by what she'd left behind, she would be happy. She couldn't wait to see Arnold's face. How she longed for the comfort of being with someone who would attend to her and love her! At last the plane landed. Teresa got her luggage and proceeded to meet the man of her dreams she would wed the following day. She looked around, saw the other passengers being picked up by their loved ones, but she didn't see Arnold yet. She figured he was just late, so she patiently waited for him to pick her up.

After twelve hours of waiting and obvious signs of distress, an airport employee approached her and asked her if she would like him to arrange transportation to her destination. She said yes. Then she gave the cab driver Arnold's address—she knew Arnold would have a worthy explanation. After all, they were to be married in the morning and there was so much to do! Her heart beating like the hooves of a wildebeest in flight, she finally arrived at his home, and although she was concerned about what had happened, she still had forgiveness in her heart and was willing to hear his explanation.

Arnold was not there. His sister lived nearby and she let Teresa stay in Arnold's house as she waited and waited. Sadly, Arnold didn't return until the evening of the day the wedding was to take place. To Teresa's horror he arrived disoriented, strung out and high on crack! It seemed he had either relapsed or had been taking drugs the whole time, but she couldn't know it until it confronted her in the face. The embarrassment, guilt and hurt that she felt at that moment emotionally paralyzed her. At that moment her life was sure to end. The devastation that overcame her was like a volcanic eruption—except her lava couldn't overflow as a way of release because her wounds, her past, her anger, her loneliness put her into a state of psychosis. Everyone had warned her, but her levees gave in and she had to confront that Katrina for herself.

The sad story of Teresa Badger is based, in part, to the real-life story of a woman who had reached her retirement years in the church and was willing to give up everything to pursue what she felt she deserved. Her wounds from her first marriage ran so deep that she spent the rest of her life seeking a replacement to heal those wounds. Her unresolved pain blinded her to what was around her. It blinded her to deal with her youngest daughter's molestation, her older married daughter's being hit on by the same man she herself wanted and also blinded her to this man's drug abuse.

Wounds that won't heal bring with them a spiritual blindness, preventing us from living the life we want to live. At this stage of Teresa's life her levees had broken and brought her to a desperate point where she was willing to walk away from her relationship with God. If her husband had told her twenty years prior that he was sorry, if her church family had helped her to resolve the pain of a failed marriage, the fall from being in a high-status family to a single-parent family, if the women she had brought into her home had respected her sincerity and kindness, those wounds could have been mended. How different Teresa's life could have been!

Wounds that won't heal require special intervention. Like Teresa Badger, many of you have done so much on your own and you are exhausted. No journaling, no writing or talking can get at those hidden sores that have putrefied all over your being. You are tired of being strong, tired of being hurt, tired of the pain. Just plain tired. There are wounds that you carry that run so deep that you have made decisions that you now regret. Those disappointments you've experienced bring such sadness, embarrassment and devastation that you don't even know where to begin to mend the wounds. You do however, may understand that you were not seeing clearly when you made certain decisions. In the void of closure for what you've been through, you have sought for love in all the wrong places. Now it is time. You may have a lot on your plate to deal with but they are all connected to those deep wounds that you know are there. You need a specialist to attend to those wounds. No more hasty decisions, no more deep reflections that replay who you could have been. It is time to heal. Jesus is the specialist you need to absolve the wounds you carry. Healing has come.

To help us understand and see how we can overcome the effects of the deep wounds we carry, I'll draw an analogy with leprosy. A contagious disease we read about in the Bible, leprosy affects the body's nervous system. The symptoms begin as numbness in the hands and feet and progress to the loss of limbs. Individuals who suffer from this disease are affected not just physically but socially. It is a disease of shame that forces the afflicted person into seclusion. A victim is usually so humiliated and frightened by their condition that they don't seek and get the treatment they need, thus allowing the disease to worsen. Although this disease is curable, the shame it brings is like a putrefying sore or wound that will not heal.

In a spiritual context, leprosy may be regarded as a form of spiritual pollution. In the New Testament are many accounts of Jesus healing lepers. In the natural sense, leprosy is the eating away of the flesh, and when compared spiritually, the disease represents our carnal nature, which creates separation with God. There is a cure for leprosy, but if you go into hiding, you can't get this cure and can't comprehend the possibilities of God healing disease, whether it is physical, emotional or mental. Jesus' healing this disease is analogous to the removal of the shame leprosy-like wounds cause. The wounds that won't heal are like a form of leprosy, but once Jesus comes on the scene you can be made whole.

So the soldiers in God's army who are ministering but not dealing with their wounds are engaged in a very dangerous battle. As a general once shared with me, "imagine a soldier with running sores or a leprosy-type condition caused by a war. This soldier cannot function at full capacity. The numbness in his hands and feet can set in at any time. So when people should be shooting their spiritual weapon, that may be the time when the numbness and tingling sets in. Maybe it has already set in with you and you can't use your firearm, so essentially you are in the army for little use.

Imagine this same soldier with the sores that now become infected. He may eventually go for treatment, but it is too late, as the sores have become resistant to treatment. Meaning, some of the wounds that people carry are at an infected stage that requires they be put in isolation and treated by a qualified specialist. All precautions have to be taken to prevent other people from getting infected by you and to prevent a church-wide pandemic" For if your bitterness spills over to another weak saint, that person will be diseased just like you.

As Isaiah says, ointment must be applied to putrefying sores. In Matthew 26:7 (KJV) it speaks of Mary Magdalene and the alabaster box:

> There came unto him a woman having an alabaster box
> of very precious ointment, and poured it on his head, as
> he sat at meat.

Mary had very expensive ointment that she poured on Jesus. Her willingness to take the most expensive possession she had and minister to the true and Living God symbolized the value of her service to God. She ignored the shame of wiping the ointment on Jesus with her hair, which is referred to as "a women's glory." Therefore her glory (hair) ministered to the Glorified One! She was certainly heckled by those around her, but she was just waiting for the right time to give that precious ointment to Jesus.

This illustrates that you have to transcend the heckling, embarrassment and hurt of the situation that has caused deep wounds and tell yourself that you will not allow the transfer of the contagious sores of denial, unforgiveness and bitterness. You must tell yourself that you have expensive oil. You have the Holy Spirit. You will use what you have and will pour it on Jesus. You will tell Him about your trouble and will pour out your oil—which is your worship of the almighty God. Like the ten lepers in Luke chapter 17 who were healed by Jesus, you can be that one who returns to give God thanks, and He will respond that "your faith hath made you whole."

It is difficult to tell somebody that God will deliver when they do not believe this is so. Therefore, for some wounds a specialist needs to be called in. A specialist is someone who can address a situation that a regular physician cannot handle. He or she is an expert trained to intervene in specific and unique circumstances. In the church, we need to tap into the spirit of counsel, for there are people there who have the gift of counselling and healing, a gift that can reach into the lives of people. The great physician, the Eternal Specialist, will treat those wounds if you come out of hiding. For wounds that won't heal can lead to other problems. They lead us to make bad decisions, enter wrong marriages and become bitter. You need to take time for yourself and understand that regardless of your age, religion or pedigree, you will not allow Katrina to come in and break your levee. Fix it now before it is too late. Don't waste the years Teresa did to sort out your life.

And finally, what do you do about the wounds that won't heal because you did not get the closure you needed to move on? I encourage you to pursue something that will improve your life. That something, my friend, lies in God. When one door closes a new one can open up for you. Jesus closed the doors of your wounds. As Isaiah 53:5 (KJV) proclaims:

> He was wounded for our transgressions; he was bruised
> for our iniquities: the chastisement of our peace was upon
> him; and with his stripes we are healed.

There is absolutely nothing that is too hard for God. A focus on the great work of Calvary will give you the strength you need to pursue the things in life you have always wanted. He was wounded so we can be set free. Seek Jesus and take your closure from him. God has prepared a future for you that will erase the wounds you thought would never heal. Jesus has already given you the closure. Your job is to step out in faith and open a new door in your life. Does a new career sound good? Maybe a new look? A ministry you have always wanted to participate in? Volunteer work for the needy? It's up to you. You know the deep potentials that lie in you. Take responsibility for your life. Seek help & be made whole. There are new doors of opportunities ahead of you waiting for you to open them, and you will never know what awaits you if you do not try.

And when you take that step and you experience the healing from God, be like that one leper who returned to give Jesus thanks. Don't wait for someone to give you closure to move on. Take your power back and take your closure in God. It is finished—and I am sorry for what you have been through. Bring those who have hurt you to God in prayer and when you do, slam that door shut!

But now ye also put off all these; anger, wrath, malice, blasphemy, filthy communication out of your mouth
(Colossians 3:8 KJV).

Chapter 6

Anger – It's Coming!

This chapter is about preparation. As you engage in real talk, appreciate the friends around you, launder your guilty stains and begin to heal from your wounds, you must be prepared for what is to come. In this journey of exposing your hidden truths, you must be mindful of the emotion we call anger. You may find that as soon as you've made up your mind to press forward and not allow your personal circumstances to keep you down, *bang!* a situation arises that can cause you to lose all you have worked for. Preparation is about being ready and anticipating the enemy's plan to thwart your deliverance amidst the great things God has in store for you.

Have you ever been so angry that you know if you give in to that emotion, you will surely lose your family, job or even freedom? Have painful life events made you so angry you can't move on until you get revenge? Then what, really, is the emotion we call anger and how does a good Christian deal with it? By definition, anger is a profound sense of displeasure. It comprises deep frustration, dissatisfaction, the sense of being wronged and hurt with faulty reasoning. Anger is an emotion we all experience in life, and if we don't have the discipline to temper it, it can make us do wrong.

There are different *types* of anger, too. For example, there is the anger we experience when we see needless suffering in our world such as famine and disease, or the anger we direct at a government that repeatedly hikes taxes without considering the negative impact on low-income families. There is also the anger that results from being abused when all you want is to see the abuser dead. There are so many situations that can make an individual legitimately angry, but if a child of God leaves anger unchecked, the outcome can be devastating.

A good way to tell the "saints" from the "aint's" is to get them angry. The enemy knows this and often throws things your way to conjure up this unpredictable emotion of anger. You would be shocked to hear what comes out of some church folks' mouths when situations arise that make them angry. I can remember being in the company of a Christian friend when a chair accidentally fell on her toe. The word that came out of her was what you might hear on a basketball court when there's a foul, a word, needless to say, that cannot be written in these pages. Now, she did sing in the choir and her voice was glorious, but the word she uttered that day was in no way glorious. Did the chair that fell on her toe make her legitimately angry? Certainly. But the *degree* of her anger in reaction to that small event revealed her hidden true nature. We should never be angry to the point that we lose control and filthy words or swearing come out of our mouths. There are two Scripture references that support this point:

> Let no corrupt communication proceed out of your mouth, but that which is good to the use of edifying, that it may minister grace unto the hearers (Ephesians 4:29, KJV).

> But now ye also put off all these; anger, wrath, malice, blasphemy, filthy communication out of your mouth (Colossians 3:8, KJV).

These passages essentially speak about the power of discipline, which is training yourself to *purposely* respond when your emotions begin to get out of control. Most times when curse words come to mind, hateful thoughts of vengeance and retaliation follow, and that is the point where we have already sinned. It is best to follow what Peter tells us:

> And beside this, giving all diligence, add to your faith virtue; and to virtue knowledge; and to knowledge temperance; and to temperance patience; and to patience godliness; and to godliness brotherly kindness; and to brotherly kindness charity (2 Peter 1:5-7, KJV).

In these verses, Peter outlines the attributes that every Christian should seek. Temperance is an essential virtue that helps the Christian to deal with anger. Temperance is self-control or the discipline you exercise to counteract the enemy's plot to push you out of balance. This discipline is best achieved through an intense and honest prayer life that puts you in a submissive state for God to speak to you. You will often find that in the heat of anger, if you take it to God, your anger will dissipate and you will find yourself in a situation where you can hear direction from Him. If you deal with anger in the absence of prayer, you leave yourself open to the desire for vengeance. As Matthew 5:44 (KJV) says,

> …Love your enemies, bless them that curse you, do good to them that hate you, and pray for them which despitefully use you, and persecute you.

This is definitely easier said than done but an active prayer life can get you through those difficult moments. It doesn't mean your anger is unfounded, but the discipline of prayer helps you to manage that anger so you are not consumed with hatred and the desire for vengeance.

If you possess the virtue of temperance that Peter talks about, you will be better prepared not to let your guard down so easily when new situations confront you. Living with temperance gives you the knowledge that God is able to fight every one of your battles. Your faith in God helps to remind you of who God is and how far He has brought you. Therefore, your anger will still be felt, but will also be brought into subjection to God's will for your life.

The Lord acknowledged that we would be angry sometimes in our Christian walk; we have to be watchful, however, and not to fall into Satan's traps. The saint goes through much within the church and probably feels it's legitimate to tell someone off or bear someone malice. But the glee you may feel from acting on your anger is often fleeting. No sooner have you satisfied your desire for revenge than you experience regret for what you have done! You may find yourself having to step back and retract what you have said, make apologies for your conduct and reconcile yourself not only with people but with God.

Consider the number of people sitting in prisons today who wish they had not given in to their anger and were still free. Sometimes the way you react to things can actually make things worse and have a lasting impact on others. Do not underestimate your Adamic nature, for it constantly seeks to be fed with ungodly actions. To live in the spirit and walk in the spirit is no easy task. Yet we can be confident that if we follow the principles of Romans 8:1, which tell us that we will not be condemned if we walk not after the flesh but after the spirit, that we can discipline our angry emotions and make the right choices.

If you lack the ability to control your anger, chaos will inevitably follow; this inability is all the enemy needs to push your speeding train off the tracks. Though you may want to curse or physically harm someone who has harmed you or a loved one, you must surrender your ideas of vengeance to God for Him to deal with. If you put things in God's hands and wait long enough, the outcome is always better than the one that results when you try to fight your battles on your own. You may hold firmly to anger because you believe that the individual who caused you harm will get away with it. You don't believe that the person will get their just reward, and so in a spirit of vigilantism, you become consumed with ensuring that vengeance is done. Unbeknownst to you, however, an unseen eye is watching; nothing is hidden from God. Every unjust act will receive its just reward. This is why your faith has to be unrelenting and you have to know what the word of God says. You have to know in whom you believe. It's best to believe in God and trust that He will take care of all things. As the song says,

> But I know whom I have believed,
> and am persuaded that He is able
> to keep that which I've committed
> unto Him against that day.

If you discipline your mind in this way, God will take care of all you have passed through; you can sit back and watch Him work. But do *not* sit back in pride, saying, "Yes, they are going to get what they deserve." No! The way you think things should be handled is usually never the way God works things out. You should sit back, not waiting to see God's retribution, but rather waiting to see the wonderful things He has in store for you. If you rest on the promises of God, you'll be able to release your anger about the injustices that you have experienced. God will do the rest and show you what steps you need to take.

We see the most anger in people who have issues of their past they have not yet resolved. Such persons may become easily provoked, suspicious of others, have compulsive behaviour, are confrontational and lack forgiveness. As previously mentioned, there are certainly legitimate reasons to feel angry, but we should not carry our anger into a new day without resolving the issues behind it. The Bible says:

> Be ye angry, and sin not: let not the sun go down upon
> your wrath (Ephesians 4:26, KJV).

This passage tells us that we should not sin when we are angry and we should not allow our anger to be prolonged. This is because anger can lead to bad choices, physical assaults and even murders. Sin that results from your anger can make you lose so much ground with God that you become too discouraged to rebuild your walk with Him. You have to hold to your faith in God, and regardless of how difficult the situations are that you face, you must ask the Lord to keep you in His will and to prevent you from making mistakes you will later regret.

The story of Sarah and Hagar in Genesis Chapter 16 is a good example of an angry person taking matters into her own hands. As the Bible explains, Sarah was barren and desperately wanted to have a child for Abraham. She resorted to her own measures, not knowing that God already had a plan for her life. Sarah told Abraham that since she was unable to produce a child for him, he should go and sleep with her servant Hagar so she could bear a child for him. Abraham agreed. Hagar conceived and had a child for Abraham just as Sarah intended. However, this didn't appease the longing Sarah had to be a mother. Ishmael, Hagar's son, was a reminder of the son that Sarah could not bear and this angered her. In Genesis 21, Sarah finally conceived Isaac as a fulfillment of a prophecy. When Isaac was weaned, Sarah told Abraham that Ishmael was mocking her son and would never share in Isaac's inheritance. Sarah despised Hagar and her son, and she went to Abraham to have them removed from their house.

Today we can see that Sarah's actions were spurred on by anger and jealousy. If Sarah had known she would eventually bear a son, she would not have asked Abraham to sleep with Hagar and thus produce a son. And then, the more than a thousand-year-long dispute in the Middle East, and particularly in Israel, would not have occurred. The descendents of Ishmael and Isaac would not have been engaged in a bloody war in which they both claimed land that was once Abraham's. If Sarah had waited on God and not taken matters into her own hands, our world would have looked very different today.

There is also a different side to anger that we should consider. Addressing anger can be a very healthy exercise for an individual. For too long, the culture of the church has been one of not adequately dealing with anger when a dispute arises. Because we are "spiritually" driven to do the right thing when situations confront us, we tend to push them aside as if nothing happened. If individuals pass through difficult life events circumstances and there is no evidence of their being angry at about the outcomes, you should see huge red flags. For when you are not angered by bad things that happen, you are living in denial of what you've been through. It is never healthy not to address anger because you are afraid of how others will react. Denying what has happened to you or a loved one is simply shelving things for another day. If you avoid being angry at obvious injustices in your life, if you repress your emotions, you're like a pressure cooker that represses heat, and if the lid is removed before the steam is released, the results are disastrous. So the *experience* of anger is an important part of healing. There is something to be processed within the circumstances that made you angry, and the act of processing it can help you to recognize situations as they really are.

A display of anger helps you to release that anger at being wronged. It also teaches lessons about boundaries and equips you to not to allow yourself to be confronted with similar situations again. Setting boundaries has to do with maintaining a healthy distance from situations or people that can trigger unwanted emotions of pain, confusion and anger. Boundaries are rules for yourself so you will not do things that can trigger negative behaviour. A smoker, for example, can set a boundary by deciding not to go out for breaks with colleagues who smoke at work, as this could reawaken the thirst for nicotine. In other words, shun the very appearance of things that could compromise your integrity. This is why when you have been wronged and you *know* you have been wronged it takes a lot of fortitude and maturity not to resort to retributive behaviour. Set your boundaries and let God be your ultimate avenger.

When you are angry, you must process the experience with God's word. The way you feed your mind has a lot to do with how your spirit will react to any negative circumstances in your life. As the saying goes, you are what you eat. It is important to feed your spirit with positive things that can help you live victoriously when issues around you are not so good. Examples of spiritual food are gospel songs, your Bible and Christian books. They can help to feed your spirit and soul so that you can deal positively with whatever comes your way. Wash yourself daily with the word of God and honest prayer. Ask the Lord to condition your mind to hear His voice so you can pray through any situation till you get your release.

Moses was one of the greatest patriarchs who ever lived. Yet in all his miraculous experiences, he did not see the Promised Land, because he'd shown such righteous indignation toward the children of Israel. Numbers Chapter 20 speaks of the arrival of the children of Israel to the desert of Zin. Moses had freed them from enslavement under Pharaoh and he had taken them on a journey to the land God had promised. The children of Israel were tired, weary and thirsty. As a result, Moses was given a direct commandment to speak to a rock so that his people could get water out of it. But Moses was angry because of their ungratefulness—they had grumbled and quarreled with him, saying it would have been better if he had left them in Egypt where they were assured of food and water. Moses, however, knew how difficult it had been to free them from slavery, and he may have felt they did not deserve water because of their lack of gratitude for what God had done for them. So in his anger he struck the rock two times with his rod, instead of speaking to the rock as the Lord had commanded. Moses' anger and subsequent disobedience resulted in him not attaining the promised land which he had worked so hard for.

His anger is understandable. But a command had been given. His story shows us that regardless of how angry we become, we still have to conduct our lives in a particular way. Let this lesson of Moses' anger be in the mind of every believer. Many actions we take that have been fueled by our anger are irreversible. It's best to allow God to govern your responses when you're angry, for there are great things at stake. Moses' punishment seems so severe, but it shows us how serious God is about not allowing our anger to get ahead of us. When you experience anger, be cognizant of how this emotion can lead you to make wrong decisions and choices. You may feel your anger is legitimate, but the way you deal with it can affect the future in ways you can not even comprehend. Train yourself to talk to the Lord and ask Him how to respond.

To keep your anger in check, you must remind yourself of who you are and how hard you've worked to be where you are—and then how long it will take for you to get back to that place if you let your anger dictate your actions. When Barack Obama was campaigning for the American presidency, he exemplified the discipline and focus one must have to reach a goal. He did not allow the deceitful things that were said about him to push him off track. He fought his presidential race with calm and an unstinting drive for excellence. Obama may have reflected on the thousands of African Americans who fought for his freedom and the slaves who built the White House awaiting his prophetic arrival, and he may have imagined the sweat that streamed down the brows of the blacks who were enslaved as they dreamed of freedom.

Obama perhaps realized that the verbal assaults and accusations made about him during the presidential race campaign could not even remotely compare to what his forefathers and predecessors had had to endure. Thus, Obama pressed on to his intended goal, doubtless aware that his conduct, if perceived negatively, could affect future black presidential contenders. He remained vigilant, strong and disciplined in order to meet his goal. He may have experienced anger at times, which I'm almost certain he did, but his discipline paid off once he became the first African-American president of the United States. And soon after he claimed the presidency, he appointed Hillary Rodham Clinton, his once vicious contender, to the office of secretary of state. Regardless of how the world may regard that move, Obama exemplified the power of discipline, integrity and keeping focused on a goal even with opposition. His decision to put Clinton in that position must be what the following passages in Proverbs actually mean:

> When a man's ways please the LORD, he maketh even his enemies to be at peace with him (Proverbs 16:7, KJV).

> Rejoice not when thine enemy falleth, and let not thine heart be glad when he stumbleth (Proverbs 24:17, KJV).

> If thine enemy be hungry, give him bread to eat; and if he be thirsty, give him water to drink (Proverbs 25:21, KJV).

Obama did not have to put Clinton in his administration, especially after the hurtful things she had said about him, but his doing so made a profound statement to the world. The example Obama set helps us to understand a spiritual application. The Scripture says that the children of God are a special people:

> But ye are a chosen generation, a royal priesthood, a holy nation, a peculiar people; that ye should shew forth the praises of him who hath called you out of darkness into his marvellous light (1 Peter 2:9, KJV).

When you know who you are and that you are part of a royal priesthood, a holy nation that is called to exemplify Christ, allow nothing to get in the way of this assured reality. You are God's special child. See your goal. Christ had a goal when he was on the cross—it was for you to be able to live a victorious life and resist Satan's plan to bring you into bondage. You may have experienced pain and trials that are unimaginable, but be resolute and see your life on the pages of God's history book. Hold to your integrity and allow nothing to distract you from your bright future. Barack Obama had a great destiny before him, and many did not believe he would be able to meet it. Yet despite the decades that preceded him, decades when black people in America had to struggle for equality with whites, Obama's anger was made glad on his inauguration day of January 20, 2009.

Barack Obama is just one example of the earthly rewards of this life. We are all part of a greater priesthood that is unmatched in this earthly realm. As God's children, we are seeking a greater inauguration day, and that is a life of eternity where God has prepared a place for us. Remember what you have gained and don't jeopardize the great strides you have made and worked so hard for. Just your reading the pages of this book is evidence that you are working through the situations in your life and perhaps thinking through some of the issues you may confront in the future. Don't throw everything away in an act of anger when you are confronted with your next trial. Life in the new pew is not easy. Be prepared and ready for what is to come. Your future is bright and there is a great inauguration day awaiting you.

LORD, you are searching for honesty. You struck your people, but they paid no attention. You crushed them, but they refused to be corrected. They are determined, with faces set like stone; they have refused to repent (Jeremiah 5:3 NLT).

Chapter 7

Let Honesty Be Your Guide

This chapter is about the importance of honesty and may serve as a guide for true Christian living. By being honest about the private pains we experience in public pews, we can begin to resolve the many issues we have ignored for too long. As Christians, it is important that we be honest about our relationship with the Lord in every step of our Christian journey. This journey is not always easy and you certainly will have some good days and some bad days. You may even have relapses and failures, but do not act as if everything is okay when you do. Be real, and resolve that no matter what you go through, you will stay with God! If you are honest about where you are at and resolute in going all the way with Jesus, then He can help you through your trials to the honour and glory of His name.

Jesus asked Peter the question "Who do men say that I am?" Direct this same question to yourself. Do you know who you really are? In other words, what have you been called to do? What is your purpose on this earth? You really cannot answer this question until you go through certain things in life and your character is proven. Many trials come to purge your life of negativities so that your positive attributes can shine for God. As Malachi 3:3 (KJV) says,

> And he shall sit as a refiner and purifier of silver: and he shall purify the sons of Levi, and purge them as gold unto silver that they may offer unto the Lord an offering in righteousness.

What you've been through can press you out of measure, but an honest heart toward God will refine you, purge you and build you into the vessel He wants you to be. As 1 Peter 1:7 (KJV) also says,

> That the trial of your faith, being much more precious than of gold that perisheth, though it be tried with fire, might be found unto praise and honour and glory at the appearing of Jesus Christ.

According to Peter, your trials are more precious than gold, because those who can survive their trials and remain committed to serving the Lord have a special place with Him. The church is filled with broken people, and many of those who have experienced private pain in public pews have not gone on record to declare how God has healed their wounds or helped them through difficult situations. It would seem, at times, that the church is filled with much dysfunction, and no one is being delivered by the hand of the Almighty. If some would give their real-talk testimony and be honest about where God has pulled them from, we would see not only tragedies and failures in the pews, but their endless victories.

It is time that we begin to be honest about what God has delivered us from so that others who are struggling can take courage. If you have remained in the church in spite of the troubles you have been through, you are amongst the remnants of those who are called to give back in some way. The church needs some honest members who can tell other abused victims that if God can clean up wretches like they, He certainly can do the same for them.

Being honest about who you really are may include pulling out the measuring stick to see where you stand in being spiritually healed. Nobody knows you like you. Until you own up to the fact that there are some things you struggle with, you will never be able to rid yourself of the pain that comes from those struggles. To be honest about your life, you have to acknowledge your struggles. It makes no sense coming to church Sunday after Sunday wearing a façade.

An area we in the church need to be honest about is the prevalence of undiagnosed mental illness. Whether we want to believe it or not, many church folk suffer from this condition. For example, one woman in the church struggled with bipolar disorder, often called manic depression, for many years. A person who is bipolar experiences extreme mood swings; one day, the sufferer can be as happy as a clam, and the next day, plunged into deep despair.

This woman was repeatedly told to pray about her depression and not give in to the devil's voice. She had struggled throughout her life with depression to the point that she had attempted suicide on several occasions. She was a churchgoer and very successful in her professional life, but she would find herself from time to time not being able to break the negative thoughts that enveloped her. What she experienced in the church, however, were the repeated prayer room visits where the devil was rebuked out of her only to soon find herself back in the depression spiral. Don't get me wrong, demonic possession is very real and I have seen many instances in my lifetime. However, we need to increase our knowledge of mental illness and adopt various ways we can deal with sufferers. If we are not equipped, we should refer such individuals to professionals so they can get the help they need.

If we're honest with each other, we must realize that we haven't accepted the fact of serious mental health issues among church members. We are well versed in spiritual warfare, but not in the warfare that begins in the mental realm. Some people periodically feel sad and depressed, but over time they naturally shake it off. This is not the mental condition I am speaking of. There are people who experience profound sadness and anxiety that cannot be easily shaken off. These feelings affect their daily routines, employment and family life. If not understood in context and counteracted, debilitating sadness, despair and anxiety are often the early stages of a very serious mental health condition.

Clinical depression, as depression may become, serves to disconnect sufferers from their ultimate purpose on earth and their sense of worth as human beings. One of the missing tools of some secular counsellors is that they don't connect individuals to their spiritual purpose. The Holy Spirit, which dwells in the life of a believer, is what connects that person to the eternal God, thus giving them hope and purpose in this life. On the other hand, a weakness of some Christian counsellors is their tendency to minimize the very real illness that can impair one's mind. If the mind is weak or has been broken by tragic events in a person's life, that person may have more difficulty than others separating illusion from the realms of reality.

The brain is a complex part of our human anatomy that must be taken care of in order for the mind to be healthy, just as a healthy body requires healthy eating. The private pains that individuals experience have been silenced for so long that the mental state of some has deteriorated and become chronic to the point of physical and mental illnesses. Just as treating cancer in its early stages can make a person cancer-free, catching the early signs of depression can have a positive result. For those who struggle with depression, a situation that only adds to their depression can literally drive a person crazy, for just as there are stages of cancer, there are stages of depression. If we continue to ignore signs of depression in people and foster an environment that does not deal with it, our pews can have ever-increasing numbers of people with this condition.

Depression is not from God. It is a spirit from the enemy that is used to drown the saint in misery, hopelessness and despair. It is a satanic lie that pushes the belief that there is no eternal hope and destiny. We must recognize the enemy's tactics. If he can prolong the symptoms of depression in people to the stage where they feel squeezed out of their spiritual vitality, I believe that is the point that physiological changes to the human brain and body occur.

This is why we should never be irritated by another person's praise and worship. The woman with the four kids as discussed in Chapter 2 was a woman who had a "crazy praise". But contrary to the church whisperings, her worship was a form of therapy. Her worship made her feel better; it gave her the strength to face her difficult circumstances. Many saints who have experienced depression have not had to go on medications like Prozac, because when they come to the house of God, their spirit is nurtured by their praise, and when you praise God and enter into worship, you are plugging yourself into God's presence, His mind and His healing power. It is in worship where He reminds the saints that "Greater is He that is within you than he that is in the world" (John 4:4). Our praise is our power. Our worship is our warfare. Despite the mental state of people you may feel do a crazy-sounding praise, like the woman with the four kids, it can be what you need to get through from day to day.

Praise and worship are important, but their practice does not mean that we shouldn't be educated in how the church can deal with depression and other mental illnesses. We tend to address what we understand and ignore what we don't understand. We need to be honest as a church community and recognize that people in the pew come from all walks of life and present different problems. That is not to say we should treat these saints the way the medical establishment would treat them—that is, medicate them—but we should provide the necessary supports. And in very serious cases, if medical intervention is needed, the saint should not be left to feel guilty about the course of action he or she must take.

It is far better that we refer people in pain to screened secular counsellors than have them remain in our pews with no intervention. The increasing number of pew members who sit amongst their abusers, or amongst those who have betrayed them, or amongst those who lied to them or had affairs with them with no resolve, only serves to worsen the health of the church today. How can we expect to have healthy pew members when the environment they come to Sunday after Sunday is not healthy?

We must begin to equip ourselves to deal with the serious problems that continue to present themselves. Take, for instance, the church sisters who have struggled with postpartum depression. We celebrate the gift of new life with them, but many of us are unaware that some, unable to endure the pressures of motherhood, harbour serious thoughts of harming their newborns. It is only by the grace of God that most of them do not follow through with such thoughts. Many of these same church sisters struggle with depression later on in their lives, and they need a positive environment where they won't feel scared and embarrassed to seek help.

In my adult life, I often reflect on the time when I was a young girl, that a man in the church committed suicide, leaving a wife and children. This man was a church member, but he had somehow slipped under the radar. I remember quite vividly the disgrace within the church community over how something like this could have happened. All the sermons he had heard in church, all the spiritual singing, couldn't drown his depression, and so he hanged himself. I remember the event so well because I was on the scene the day after it happened. I had to go with my mother when she went to comfort the man's widow. I remember wanting badly to go back upstairs when family members of the deceased gave us a tour of the basement where the man had hanged himself. But I knew it was best to stick close to my mother—that was the safest place to be at that time.

My mother was one of many who expressed their condolences to the widow as I sat by. Maybe in those days, parents didn't realize that children should not be in such a setting—I mean, what was my mother thinking? That event traumatized me for years. I was scared to go into basements because the image of how this man had hanged himself in one was engraved on my mind, and remains there even to this day.

I listened to the adults who asked why he had taken his own life. As a child, I asked the same question—what could be so bad that he would want to leave this world? The answer that was given, which I will keep confidential, lets me know today that there is so much more to that story. Today I speculate that the man may have had a mental illness. Nobody wakes up one morning, decides to end his life and carries through with it for the reasons circulating at that time. I remember people in the church declaring they had had dreams about this man in the weeks before he took his life, but the sad thing is that no one acted on his silent scream in time.

Many in the church struggle with sporadic thoughts of suicide. They think about how they would do it and how others would feel if they did. Thank God, most have been rescued from these thoughts through the supernatural healing power of Jesus. The gospel has changed many lives, and many of you can testify to having had thoughts of suicide but the word of God and His message of hope saved you. Still, some continue to struggle. Some have attempted suicide and returned to the pews unnoticed.

As much as the church may be inclined to resist the reality of mental illness, we can no longer do so. Let us begin to look around us and be honest about what we see. Who doesn't look happy today? Who are we overlooking? Are there any humble Helens nearby? Is there a Samantha who is trying to overcome her history of sexual abuse? Or maybe a Linda who has been mistreated by her church brethren? And perhaps a Cindy and Tracey who have been played by a church pimp? Who around you needs a word of encouragement that just might break the cycle of despair in their lives?

We are living in very serious times. We cannot afford to pretend that things are just peachy keen. There are people in our churches with schizophrenia, and bipolar and anxiety disorders, just as there are people with diabetes, cancer and AIDS. We need only to open our eyes, see who amongst us is suffering and start a dialogue about how we can help; in other words, change the complacent attitude of the church. If we don't, too many people will slip under the radar, only to be heard of again when tragedy strikes.

God has been with us every step of our journey and we are beginning to learn a bit more about who we really are. We will come to appreciate where God has brought us as we understand the paths He has made for us to walk through. God has brought us through our experiences and it is important that we continue to be honest and true. Psalms 51:6 (KJV) says:

> Behold, thou desirest truth in the inward parts: and in the hidden part thou shalt make Me to know wisdom.

To get to know yourself better, list the five traits you have that you want to change (e.g., I am negative):

I am_____

I am_____

I am_____

I am_____

I am_____

Now, change each statement to things you want to be (e.g., I want to be friendlier):

I want to be_____

I want to be_____

I want to be_____

I want to be_____

I want to be_____

Honesty, as they say, is the best policy. By writing the things you want to be rather than who you have been, can help you to maintain honesty. You will never lose out when you are honest about yourself. So when you are confronted with hard situations in life, stand your ground and ask God, What are you teaching me? What do you want to change in me and how can I use it to be a better person?

Honesty requires deep reflection. It requires you to be sincere and genuine. Be honest about what is really troubling you. Don't pretend you have a headache when what you really have is a bellyache. Honesty about your true situation is the most liberating thing you can do. Being honest about what has happened in your life is like removing the excess weight from your emotions. Jesus knows us all and He knows best what we need to work on in life so that we can move through the proper healing processes that stop the negative cycles in our lives. Be honest, true and be made whole. A life in God is waiting for you. Your pains of yesterday will not be your tomorrows.

When you are recalling events in your life that bring on negative feelings, don't edit the true circumstances. Often, when we think we are ready to be honest, we replay only what we are comfortable saying, avoiding things that embarrass us. We sift through the information of our lives like an editor who makes changes to a manuscript to make it easier to read. Consider the following scriptures:

> Honesty guides good people; dishonesty destroys treacherous people (Prov.11:3 NLT).

> And my honesty will testify for me in the future... (Genesis 30:33 NIV).

As these passages encourage you, let honesty be your guide. Let honesty be a guide to true Christian living, the sort that promotes health and well-being for the total person.

In home and garden shows on television, we hear a lot these days about the need to de-clutter. Take this literally in your personal life. Just as you purge the closets in your home, purge the closets of your past. The memories, hurts and disappointments that plague your mind take up too much space—you need to de-clutter. Practically, you will need to make changes in your life to rid your mind of clutter. For example, if you are coming out of sins of the flesh, any reminders of who you have been with need to be destroyed. This may mean gifts you have received, clothes, emails or text messages you may have received—discard them all! Then you are ready for a cleanup of any psychological clutter—for example, troubling memories that keep you in a state of guilt, sadness, anger or fear. You must break certain cycles in your life and claim your mind back to serving the Lord as you should.

Ridding your life of negative clutter is about making the choice to be free from situations that keep you down. Your honesty allows you to act on the understanding that you are always a target for Satan. There is clutter you must rid yourself of in order to be delivered and healed from a situation. Just because you have broken off a sexual relationship with a married man five years ago, for example, does not mean you can work with him on the Sunday school board today. You may think you are strong, but as the scripture says in 1st Corinthians 10:12 (KJV),

Let him that thinketh he standeth take heed lest he fall.

Be wise about the choices you make from here on forward. There is certainly a lot to process in the pages of this book and in our lives, but with God all things are possible. The church is a place we have all come to love. For many, church is our life and, frankly, there is no other place we would rather be. The paradox is that in all the twists, turns and pains pew members endure, the church is still our community and our source of help. The best thing we all can do is remain on the potter's wheel and be honest about the conditions around us.

Let's get it together, people! The church is a wonderful place. Let's begin to be open and honest about what we need to deal with, so deliverance can be ours.

Forget what happened in the past, and do not dwell on events from long ago (Isaiah 43:18 GWT).

But forget all that, it is nothing compared to what I am going to do (NLT Isaiah 43:18).

Chapter 8

When They Know Your Past

So here you are! What a journey. We now have a better understanding of how things affect pew members. We've defined "real talk" for pew members, appreciated our friends, absolved the guilty stains, told our wounds to let us go, begun preparation so that anger doesn't get the best of us, and we will strive to use honesty to guide us on this Christian journey. Now that we have exposed some of the things hidden in the pews, we want to conclude by rethinking the ways we react to pew members when we know their past failures and mistakes. We also want to break free of the paralysis that grips us when others say things about our own past, and move on to victory and complete deliverance.

It is important that we understand that not everyone who has been in a mess will stay in a mess. When we know someone's past, it is vitally important that we do not dwell on that past. Because the exercise of exposing the secret things that go on in the pews is not about airing dirty laundry, but rather about ushering in the emotional healing that is needed in the body of Christ today.

People in the church experience pain just like anybody else. The only distinction is the saving grace of Christ our Lord, which empowers pew members to live for Christ in spite of what they have been through. I believe that we all have a testimony that is difficult to share, and that is why, when we know people who have publicly or privately struggled with their past, their testimony should never be used against them. Instead, we should think of our own past struggles and muse on the mercy of Jesus that has kept us thus far. We must encourage those around us to be resolute in the belief that God can see them through their trials. I pray that the words on the pages of this book will encourage you, and every pew member, to release the past that holds one back from the destiny God has created.

Have you ever had the experience of knowing someone as a baby or a child, and then you move away and return many years later to find that same baby or child is now an adult? Do you find that you are shocked by how different that person looks, how much they have grown and how much they have progressed in life? Your shock is because the image of them imprinted on your mind is the one you had when you left all those years before, and that image has not caught up to their current reality. You may find it difficult to accept them as an adult, and in some instances, you still treat them like a child, because the image you had of them prevents you from trusting and accepting who they are now. In this situation, we have to understand that regardless of what we remember that child to be, they have passed through the life stages of infancy, childhood and adolescence to adulthood, and they are now, in fact, adults and should be treated like such.

This simple example helps us to understand that we should not refuse to accept someone's current reality because of a belief we've held in the past about them. Treating the grown-up child just as we did the child is precisely what many of us do in the church today. You may know about someone's past failures or stigmas, and many years later you are still defining them by their past! The fact is, what happened in the past may have nothing to do with who God says they are now. Yet every time you see them direct the choir, come to church every other Sunday, deliver a sermon or help out in church administration, you still have those negative images in your head. Yes, we are human and will remember things that have occurred in the past, but we need to re-train the way we think and focus on the saving grace of God that transcends a person's past mistakes and problems. For while we are judging someone based on their past, that someone has matured and may have moved on in complete deliverance through the power of Jesus! All individuals with broken pasts can later become whole through God, so that they can carry out His mandate.

It is unfortunate that our minds tend to focus on the negative experiences of church folk more than they focus on the positive. This has to do with our lack of faith that God can do wonderful things in a life that was previously wounded. Just knowing someone's past can serve to disconnect us from the awesome possibilities of God. It also enforces a negative image of the church that says no one can live a true life for Christ. Our minds can be a whirlwind where negative thoughts and memories battle for top position. But as God admonishes us in Philippians 2:5 (KJV),

Let this mind be in you, which was also in Christ Jesus.

A mind of Christ embraces the notion that there is hope for the fallen soul. If the church does not give hope to those in pain and turmoil, it has lost its mandate. Where there is no hope there is no future, and the truth of God is exchanged for a lie. People need to come to the realization that regardless of their pain, brokenness or troubled pasts, there is a place they can turn to for healing their mind, soul and spirit.

It is also important that we not judge the church through a lens of perfection. People in the church are not perfect and they have proclivities and difficulties just like anyone else. The imperfections that we all share are part of the human struggle. The redemption of Christ is really a paradox that every Christian should understand. When the perfect Jesus died for the sins of the world, His act became a statement to Satan that anyone who comes to Jesus, no matter their earthly imperfections, can be helped. The saint will one day be perfected when Christ returns to give eternal life to all his believers. Satan lost his chance. His accusations against the saint are about vengeance—vengeance for what he, Satan, lost—and he will do everything he can to subvert God's plan for all humankind. For *Satan's* plan is to displace humankind from the destiny that he lost. We are all in this race together and we have to keep in mind what this race is all about.

Your knowledge of someone's past is not there for you to embalm and keep set in your mind—this only serves to imprison God's people. The time you spend musing about someone's past is time you should be spending on your own. Only someone who has no appreciation for life and the awesome power of God has time to gloat about another's past mistakes and failure. Doing so, in effect keeping the person hostage, is akin to saying that the atoning blood of Christ cannot make them new again. The sooner we understand that we have been pulled from our own dark pasts is the sooner we can appreciate what God can really do in another life. Even the most wounded soldier can overcome his injury and be the exact vessel God is looking for.

If you feel locked down because everyone knows your business and you feel that your image will never be repaired, you are essentially denying the saving grace of God. One of the most important ingredients for success in a Christian life is faith. If you comb through the scriptures, God always rewards people who have faith in him. This is because faith comes by hearing the word of God and not by seeing (Romans 10:17, KJV).

So often we base the outcome of situations on what we see. Just as you can be shocked at seeing the child who grew up in your absence, your sight cannot appreciate the growth that took place. Although you didn't *see* this maturation, it went on regardless. Faith allows your spirit to witness what your eyes cannot. It may seem obvious to the eye that nothing good can come out of a particular set of circumstance, but faith in God puts out a challenge. It's a challenge a person receives to make things, despite their troubled past, undergo a positive turnaround.

If you firmly believe, as the scripture says, that God is able to do exceedingly abundantly above whatever you ask or think (Ephesians 3:20), I promise you that your faith will bring you out of the darkness. There is absolutely nothing too hard for God. So don't focus on the wrong thing. Don't waste time worrying about what others are saying or thinking about you. Don't bother investigating who said what about you, for you will never reach a conclusion that satisfies you. Our perceptions of what people say or think about us is the number-one reason people do not fulfill the calling of God in their lives. We get too taken up with what people think about us, rather than God.

People cannot save you—only God has the power to do that. Just as you would shout hoorahs for your basketball star or favourite tennis player to win a match, you should be rooting for your fellow pew member, regardless of his or her past. We must see the good in people, rather than the bad, for this is how Jesus sees us. He told Israel in Jeremiah 29:11, (KJV):

For I know the thoughts that I think toward you, saith
the LORD, thoughts of peace, and not of evil, to give you
an expected end.

We should not see pew members the way the devil wants them to be
seen, because their being constantly reminded of situations they've escaped
from makes it very difficult for them to move on. It also makes it difficult
for them to engage in real talk, for they know how church members may
think about them if they do. This is why we need to be delivered *from* what
people say about us. We need to adjust our thinking and understand that
people do grow, repent and reconcile themselves to God. So train your
mind to consider the possibility that a person has moved away from sin,
past failures and traumas, and instead think positively about who that
person can become in God.

Never make the mistake of judging someone based only on their past.
Their struggles or mistakes only make up a part of them. The Bible teaches
us that our future is meant to be brighter than our past. Consider Paul, the
persecutor of the church, who had an enlightening experience with God
on the Damascus road; or Job, who unquestionably lost everything and
became severely afflicted in his body; or David, who committed adultery
with Bathsheba and committed murder; or Rahab, who lived a life of
harlotry. All these biblical characters had difficult and tumultuous pasts,
sins they were not proud of. Their futures, however, were brighter than
their pasts, and they all became faithful servants of the Lord and received
a better reward.

In considering these biblical examples, we should always remember
that not only is there a real talk story about people's lives, but there is a real
talk story about their futures, which we may not be able to comprehend.
As onlookers, there is much we do not know. Sometimes people with
very public failures have very private episodes of deliverance. We may not
know the hard work these pew members have done to get to where they
are now, for we weren't there when God dealt with their brokenness. We
were not there!

The troubled pew member may have suffered sleepless nights, shed
buckets of tears and attempted to end life because circumstances seemed
so impossible. But this same individual trusted God. They had faith during

their quiet moments with God and could recall the healing that came from His words; they could stand by their decision never to return to the cause of their sorrow. There is so much that has gone on behind closed doors in the lives of pew members that we are not aware of it. All we may know are someone's past acts of indiscretion, but we may not be up-to-date on God's healing power in that someone's life. So consider these possibilities when you find yourself stuck in rehearsing someone's past where unbeknownst to you they have moved on.

The sooner we understand that people *can* be pulled from their dark pasts, the sooner we appreciate what God can do. When you know someone's troubled past, work earnestly to replace this negative knowledge with the positive things that can happen in Christ. If you are engaged in strong prayer and a spiritual walk with the Lord, the Holy Spirit will update you and allow you to witness the greater heights in God the person is pursuing, just as the Holy Spirit will let you know when the person is *not* engaged in such holy pursuits. This healthy attitude toward your brothers and sisters in the Lord cleans up the environment we worship in. It rids the church of the suspicion that occurs amongst pew members and, most important, puts the focus where it should be—on the victory of the cross through Christ Jesus.

If you are that individual whose troubled past is common knowledge to everyone, you must endeavour to tie your identity to Christ, rather than to church folk, for some church folk simply refuse to live the life God wants for them. Don't worry about these individuals. In every garden there are weeds that strive to hinder the growth and the beauty of the plants around them. So know that you are a flower in God's garden. You may be that tulip we spoke about in Chapter 3 that's planted in the fall, grows in winter and brings beauty only in early spring, or the perennial daylily that blooms in midsummer and does not need to be replanted as seasons change, flowering year after year regardless of the elements around it. What flower are you? Forget how you bloomed in your past season and strive to be the fresh flower that is relevant to today's tasks. The Gardener (Jesus Christ) can fertilize your soil and pluck out the weeds that choked you in the previous season. Your job is simply to trust him and have faith in him and know that beauty will come out of you in the next season.

You may ask how a dark past, such as being the victim of sexual abuse, can bring glory to God. Well, you were not supposed to make it. You were supposed to die. You were supposed to have no purpose. Yet here you are. Now *your* vessel can be used to help other afflicted souls to see beyond their pasts. A vessel is needed to let the world know that, yes, the church has private pains in public pews, but God can heal all wounds.

Let nobody but God tell you who you are and what God means to you. Refresh your mind and spirit with the realities of what God has done in your Life. Let God dictate your future, for this will help you overcome what people say about your past. Do not become the vessel that unleashes its negativity and puts a damper on your God-given purpose. When others know your past, build your future in God. Know God's voice, know your potential, and reaffirm to yourself to whom your life belongs. Do not give in to their negativities, but rather think and speak of the things that Paul said in Romans 8:35-39, (KJV):

> Who shall separate us from the love of Christ? shall tribulation, or distress, or persecution, or famine, or nakedness, or peril, or sword? As it is written, for thy sake we are killed all the day long; we are accounted as sheep for the slaughter. Nay, in all these things we are more than conquerors through him that loved us. For I am persuaded, that neither death, nor life, nor angels, nor principalities, nor powers, nor things present, nor things to come, nor height, nor depth, nor any other creature, shall be able to separate us from the love of God, which is in Christ Jesus our Lord.

Paul's faith in God was relentless. He refused to allow the pressures of this life to push him off track in his God-given destiny. You must speak life into your future, he is saying, and move toward your destiny. Your past may bring shame, but it is temporary. Your experience can keep you humble and at the feet of Jesus. Don't retreat even when they know your dirt. All that matters is that it was from the dirt of the ground that God made humankind. If God can make living souls from the dirt, He certainly can wash the dirt off you and make you into what He wants you to be.

If you feel ashamed of your past, you do not have to let this past define you. Regardless of what they know about you, make sure God knows about you in a relational way, that is, through prayer, fasting, consecration, meditation and reading the word of God. Your past is what others may focus on for their own pleasure, but understand this—that focus has more to do with *their* brokenness than yours. We all have had tough times and we should not point the finger at others. We should only reflect on how good God has been as echoed in the chorus of this hymn:

> Grace, grace, God's grace,
> Grace that will pardon and cleanse within;
> Grace, grace, God's grace,
> Grace that is greater than all our sin!

God's grace covers your past and I encourage you to make the following commitment:

> You weren't there when He found me; you weren't there when He sought me. You may know my past, but God knows my future. Therefore I am going to believe God. I am going to have faith in God. If I have faith in people I will certainly fail. So I will determine from this day forward to look to who can really help me. That is only Jesus. My spiritual bloodline carries a promised seed and soon everyone will see what my bright future will bring. I am so glad that in everything God will get His glory.

It is only when you get into the presence of God that you can commit to words like these. You get into his presence through worship, prayer and faith. In those moments your spirit will begin to reveal what God has in store for you. When you have these encounters with God, you will not hear what others have to say about you, because when *God* speaks everything is silenced.

There are no great people in the church, no people who live without sin or pain. Private pain is everywhere! But one thing is certain: there is a great God who can put great abilities in people. The greatness in you is not you. It is God's pulsating and energizing spirit that is pushing you toward his plan and distancing you from your failures. If you can just be disciplined for a little while longer, the words of naysayers will ultimately have no impact in your life.

A godly character is what God wants of all of us. A godly character means that you operate at a level that transcends what people have to say. You are resolute in your belief that God, not people, dictates your life. People may know your past, but you must walk humbly according to the dictates of the Lord. Lose that chip on your shoulder—it only prolongs your deliverance. Only at the feet of Jesus can you hear His voice and His plans for you. Be humble to His will, and though you have been tested, tried and battered, you can accept His healing and be ready to be used for God.

As you press forward and grab hold of your deliverance, I want to reiterate that people around you will not necessarily be up-to-date with the workings of God in your life. Unfortunately many pew members prefer to wallow in the negativity and so that is all they will ever see until they decide to make different choices. Whatever pain you have gone through and overcome, their negativity will shake up your environment, and often, it's why your past becomes front-page news. What I am saying is, your deliverance may present a challenge to other pew members. This challenge can be positive or negative—positive to the many who will be inspired by your upliftment and decide to follow the same path, and negative to those who resist any challenge to their inertia, apathy and stagnation.

A parallel can be drawn in the area of weight loss. If you are obese and do the work necessary to lose weight, you may find that overweight people around you react in positive or negative fashion. The positive folks embark on a journey to lose weight too, but the negative folks seem to prefer that you remain overweight so that they aren't challenged to change; when you are engaged in healthy eating, they are doing the opposite and consuming junk food. So, when you shed your past and become spiritually lighter, not everyone will be able to handle it. It shakes up their environment and destroys their complacency. But to those who prefer to remain weak and "overweight" in their emotion, you must say, please stand aside and make way for the pew members who have activated their faith and look toward a future where destiny awaits.

You may have learned a lot about yourself in ways you never dreamed of. You may have experienced the supernatural hand of God moving in your life. It is like a new birth experience for you. You see God and life in a brand-new way. When you begin the process of dealing with hidden secrets in your life, it is extremely important for your deliverance and healing that you remain steadfast. Too many times we go to the mountain top and think we are free, but the enemy recognizes that the mountain has a shaky foundation. So take your time in this process. Build your strength with constant reading of God's word, for this is how your faith can grow. The enemy recognizes when any doors have been left open for him to walk through, just as he recognizes when doors have been slammed shut.

I hope you feel lighter and encouraged by what you have read in the pages of this book. If you press toward God and have relentless faith in Him, your destiny can be free from the shackles of your past. Things will get better if they already haven't begun to do so. You can feel your strength and determine not to be enslaved by your broken past. You can see your true bloodline now, which is Jesus. Great things await you, so don't miss this roll call!

It's been awesome ministering to you in this way, and there is so much more to talk about…but my mandate is complete for now. Let this book be a reminder of God's love and favour toward those in despair. Yes, private pains do exist in our pews, but publicly we declare that if it wasn't for the grace of God, we would have been swallowed up. But thanks be to God that his saving grace has kept us this far. Walk strong and love the Lord! He will see you through. God bless you all! Till next time…

About The Author

Elaine A. Brown Spencer, Ph.D., Speaker, Counsellor, Professor, Founder & President of Kaleo Inc. is a scholar of spiritual-religious experiences. Dr. Spencer earned her undergraduate degrees in Political Science, Social Science and Social Work at York University, Toronto, Ontario, Canada. She subsequently completed her Masters of Social work and a PhD in Sociology of Education and Equity Studies at the University of Toronto, Toronto, Ontario, Canada. A professor at two Canadian universities, Elaine strives to bridge the religious and academic community in her writings to emphasize the need for persons to remain anchored in their faith, particularly in these trying times.

After being inspired by God to write a book, *Private Pain in Public Pews* was birthed. In this book, Elaine breaks the silence to some issues we've all heard about in church pews and unravels the paradoxical role of the church today.

Elaine lives in Toronto, Ontario, with her husband, Floid, and they have three children.

Notes

Notes

Notes

Notes

Notes

Notes

Notes

Notes

LaVergne, TN USA
28 October 2010

202508LV00002B/5/P